Your Simple Guide to Enjoying Your Maui
Vacation During and After Covid19 Pandemic

MAUI
2021 AND
BEYOND

Aloha Nancy,
Mahalo for your support !
♡ Liza

LIZA E. PIERCE
Foreword by Stacy Hope Small

Disclaimer

This book is designed to offer suggestions and resources for visitors to Maui. It is sold with understanding that the publisher and author are not engaged in rendering legal or professional advice or services. This book should only be used as a general guide. The purpose of this book is to entertain and educate. Neither the author or the publisher assumes any responsibility or liability on behalf of the purchaser or reader of the materials.

The viewpoints on this book are based on the author's personal experience, especially while living on Maui, Hawaii. All attempts have been made to verify the information provided by this publication. Neither the author nor the publisher assumes any responsibility for error, omissions, or contrary interpretations of the subject matter herein.

Because of the dynamic nature of the internet, any website address or link may eventually be invalid. Because of the dynamic nature of COVID-19 pandemic situation, the Hawaii Safe Travel Program and protocols may have been revised and updated.

CONTENTS

To Gardner and Noelle, may you be inspired.

And to the Maui Lovers locally and around the world. With Aloha.

FOREWORD

When Liza first shared with me that she planned to pen a guidebook to Maui focused on "2021 and Beyond", my first thought was WHO BETTER to take on this monstrous task than my dear friend Liza Pierce? Liza and I spent the entire Pandemic here on Maui, and had a front row seat to all of the changes brought on by this new version of our world.

A longtime Maui resident and one of the most-respected bloggers here locally, there is a level of trust that Maui visitors have put in Liza as they rely on her insights and photos and videos to show them the "real" Maui.

I first met Liza digitally under her twitter handle @AMauiBlog several years ago as I, like many, followed her for fun insights and advice about this magical island we adore. It was Liza's twitter feed I followed for direction on what was happening locally whenever I would visit Maui and I also followed her guidance on who else to connect with locally once I opted to make Maui my FULL-TIME home in January, 2020.

There is a plethora of so-called "Maui experts" but there is only one Liza! Well, she's often instilled doses of joy into my soul with her 'various alter-egos @visitlivelovemaui and @AuntiePineapple!

I also admire her leadership on a community Facebook page known as Visit Live Love Maui. Liza had her hands full this past year, with so many Maui lovers frustrated and even angry that they could not visit their favorite island. Those of us living here had mixed feelings, we of course, missed the buzz and economic fortitude that tourism brings to an island like Maui. But Liza and I also have a deep understanding of the culture here, and the importance of "Kamaaina First" and protecting the Ohana. The motto amongst us "locals" has become "Spread Aloha, Not Corona". I've watched with awe as Liza handled the negative comments about our home island on the Facebook page, offering up her honest opinion of why in this day and age, it's essential to stay positive and foster optimism while being kind, truthful and realist.

If you want to know what's happening here on Maui, now and into the future, then you have the RIGHT book in your hands. It should be the book you gift to anyone planning a visit to Maui in 2021 and Beyond. As a fellow author (my first book *Why Not Me?!? 12 Lessons a Year on an Island Taught me About Living my Dreams, and How you Can Live Yours, Too* is available on Amazon), I have also watched my own personal life change immensely here on Maui. I went from running a highly-successful $18 million luxury travel firm (*Elite Travel International*) to seeing that business decimated in a matter of days.

I opted NOT to leave Maui at all this entire year, but to use it as opportunity to take a break from traveling the world as I've done for the past 25 years. And, I stayed put. I flew to Maui with my three rescue dogs on January 26, 2020 and at this writing (November 25, 2020) haven't left the island. It feels safe here. I stayed home when we were told that we are "safer at home" and I rebranded my life and business brands under the digital umbrella www.stacymaui.com. I turned my healthy cookie baking hobby into a new business and also got to work on my second book, and launched a division of healing services and a VIP Maui concierge program. Like Liza, I am happiest when I am living, working and loving the local community here on Maui. Despite what's happening in the world, Maui has magical energy. It always has, it always will. Please enjoy Liza's modern-day guidebook to the Maui of today, and beyond.

Mahalo (*thank you*) and much aloha (*love*) for understanding that Living Pono (doing the right thing) is always the right thing to do whether you live here or visit Maui. This is a BIG lesson I've learned from my favorite local friends like Liza Pierce. We are all Ohana. ALOHA!

Stacy Hope Small
Maui-based Founder of Elite Travel
Author & Reiki Healer
November 25, 2020
Wailuku, HI

Note from the Author: At the time of publication, June 2021, Stacy Small is back on being busy with Elite Travel International. You may find her at https://www.stacymaui.com/elitetravel

INTRODUCTION

The year 2020 is an unforgettable year! This COVID-19 pandemic has uprooted our way of life in so many different ways. Travel is one of the things that has been heavily affected.

(This photo was taken at Kamaole Beach III on January 2020)

In March 2020, Maui was "closed". A 14-day quarantine was required for everyone coming to Maui. This was a decision made to prevent the spread of COVID-19 on this beautiful island in the Pacific.

As a result of the closure, Maui's tourism industry was adversely affected and resulted in economic devastation in the island. And yes, we know the whole world is affected, but we are going to focus on Maui, our beloved island home and how COVID-19 has affected travel here.

There were several attempts to re-open Maui (August 1st, September 1st) but due to surges, they were delayed. Thankfully, Maui re-opened on October 15, 2020!

Why is this book needed?

Maui has changed. Most Maui Guidebooks available at this time are either inaccurate or irrelevant as many businesses, especially restaurants have closed. Some of these shutdowns were temporary as they are waiting for the tourists to return, while others have permanently closed down. This book will give you the most current information available upon writing.

Who will benefit from this book?

Both new visitors and return visitors will benefit from this book.

For new visitors, this book outlines the basic things you need to know about visiting Maui. I understand how excited you are about your first visit, and I am excited for you as well. I am aware that you might want to pack a lot of activities into your first visit. That is not the best option. Proper planning is important so you don't feel like you need a vacation after your vacation. Ideally, it is best to have a relaxing and memorable Maui vacation and this book will help you achieve that. Another important aspect of this book for new visitors is to understand the culture of Maui, and Hawaiian culture in general. And last but not the least is safety. The last thing you want to happen is for an avoidable accident to occur. There are important safety precautions in this book, and those alone makes this book essential.

For returning visitors, you are already familiar with Maui. You already know the restaurants you love and plan to return to when you get back. You already know the sites you want to visit and the activities you love. What benefit would you derive from this book? There have been many changes from what you have previously experienced on Maui. This book will help you save time in researching how it has changed. It will help you plan your next visit better. Travel requirements, resorts and restaurants have changed over time (more so in this time of pandemic) and this book will be your most current and relevant guide.

Disclosures and my background

This book is not a book from traditional corporate travel publications such as Fodors, Lonely Planet or Frommers. This book is written from my own experience and knowledge based on living here on Maui for 27 years, and living on Maui during this COVID-19 pandemic. This book is written from a personal perspective and from my 15 years' experience as a Maui Blogger (www.amauiblog.com).

I have helped thousands of people plan their best Maui vacation through my blog and social media channels. I am also the founder and manager of the vibrant Facebook Group "Visit Live Love Maui" with over 13K members. This Facebook group is composed of Maui residents and visitors who are passionate about Maui. I learn a lot from the members too. Therefore, the insights from this new book are also influenced by the experiences shared by the residents and visitors on Visit Live Love Maui Group.

This book is just the beginning. To go deep on a topic, or to get the latest update, I will provide resources, such as links to websites and videos online.

This Book Is Not for You If ...

This book is not for you if you are looking for a Maui Guide with many colored photos and maps. To minimize the cost of printing and to be able to sell this book at an affordable price, I opted to add only a few black and white photos on the print version. The e-book version will have a colored photo. As for the maps, nowadays you can get the maps via Google maps and various Apps. If you prefer printed copies of map, those are available freely in many magazines you will find when you arrive at the airport on Maui. Beautiful colored photos are also available on my Instagram at @amauiblog - https://www. instagram.com/amauiblog/

This book is not for you if you are looking for in-depth reviews of hotels, condos, restaurants and activities. It is not the goal of this book to offer in-depth reviews. I simply give my commentary and a personal recommendation to family and friends when I mention a business here.

Why do we need to pay for a book when all the information we need is available on the internet?

My friends, have you ever tried searching something on Google by typing a word or a phrase, and Google gives you a lot of results, but not the ones you actually need or want? Then you try typing a new search and the results are overwhelming – many are irrelevant. Eventually you will find the answers but you ended up wasting so much time *googling*.

While I agree that answers to your questions may be found on the internet, I can assure you that you will have to spend hundreds of hours to find the concise and relevant information that you will find in this book. Furthermore, many of the articles you will find when you search the internet will be laced with marketing inserts and pop-up advertisements all around.

The amount of time you will save, and even the amount of money you will save from the tips found in the book make this book worth buying for you and loved ones, family and friends, coming to visit Maui 2021 and beyond.

With that said, *"the internet is our friend"* because this book will lead you to the best resources about Maui on the world wide web, we call the internet. The difference is instead of you searching, I will simply give you the specific web address to go to.

BOOK OUTLINE AND WHAT TO EXPECT

Chapter 1 – When Is the best time to visit Maui?

This is among the most frequently asked questions by first time visitors planning to come to Maui. You have heard the expression *"timing is everything."* When it comes to planning your Maui Vacation, timing is not everything, but I sure see it as very important.

Your reasons for coming to visit Maui varies and will affect your timing. This chapter will guide you in making the decision on when is the best time FOR YOU to visit Maui.

Chapter 2 – Where to Stay on Maui

This topic is also one of the most asked and frequently researched topics about planning a vacation on Maui. I am excited to answer this question for you.

You will notice that I will tend to talk about South Maui and West Maui more than other parts of Maui. It is because that is where most visitors stay. I will be mentioning other towns too, however, our primary focus is South and West Maui.

Molokai and Lanai are part of Maui too, but I will not be discussing them in this book except for a few mentions.

Chapter 3 – Pre-Travel Must Do, Arrival & Transportation

This chapter is written during the COVID-19 Pandemic. I am aware that changes happen quickly, and nothing is set in stone when it comes to arrival systems and procedures, so you will hear me say *"at this time of writing"* frequently in this chapter.

I will give you resources on where to find the latest information and updates since this book was published so you can double check.

This chapter is very important, both for first time visitors and repeat visitors, so do not skip this chapter when reading this book.

Chapter 4 – Where To Shop on Maui

What to do upon your arrival on Maui will include grocery shopping, especially if you are staying in a condo instead of a hotel. This chapter will help you save money. *Don't like to grocery shop on your vacation?* No problem! There are shopping delivery service options that I will discuss in this chapter.

Chapter 5 – What To Do on Maui

Finding something to do is not the problem. The problem is choosing which activities to do. There are a hundred and one options, and more! This is actually where I got stuck in my first attempt to write a Maui Guidebook. When I was first writing, I wanted this chapter to be super comprehensive. I wanted to cover everything! That was hard. So, in this book, I decided to include the highlights. I will discuss the Top Eight (8) Things to do and then will mention others but not give full details. I then will direct you to various websites for additional information. Top on the lists are beaches, sunrise and sunsets at Haleakala, the road to Hana, hiking and coastal walks, farm tours, and whale watch cruises.

Chapter 6 – Where To Eat and What To Eat in Maui

As much as Maui is known for its beautiful nature, Maui's culinary scene is also something to look forward to. The restaurant industry is one of the most seriously affected by COVID-19, so this is where all previous Travel Guides fall short. They are not current.

For repeat visitors, this chapter is the most helpful, and I'd say a must read. Because you already know Maui, some of you already have favorite places to eat. Some of them have closed (*Examples: Da Kitchen in Kahului and Aloha Mixed Plate are now closed – Da Kitchen is Kihei recently re-opened but in a smaller place, sharing with Piko Café*).

This will be a fun chapter to read, especially for the foodies. I will be sharing about Local Food, Hawaiian Plates Lunches, Food Trucks and Sweets & Treats.

Chapter 7 – Important Safety Reminders

Vacation is supposed to be a happy relaxing time. We do not want accidents and tragedies to happen during our vacation. Repeat visitors most likely know many of the reminders I will mention. However, for first time visitors, this chapter is absolutely a MUST READ. There are certain dangers unique to Maui that you need to know. A few minutes or hours invested in learning about these dangers is worth it. Knowing what to do and not to do to have a safe vacation is a life saver.

Chapter 8 – Secrets to Fully Enjoying Your Maui Vacation – Know and Understand Hawaii's Basic Culture

During my research, when I was reading many Maui travel guides, one thing I noticed is that few of the books placed emphasis on knowing Hawaii's culture and values before coming to Maui. I was surprised.

I've found that visitors who know and understand the basic Hawaiian values and cultures are the ones who enjoyed their Maui vacation to the fullest. They not only fall in love with the place, but they also fall in love with the people. It is very important to understand the basic culture of the place you are visiting, so this chapter is a "must read".

CHAPTER 1

WHEN IS THE BEST TIME TO VISIT MAUI?

Is Maui a "Safe Place" to visit during this pandemic? My answer is relatively *"Yes." Will I still enjoy my Maui vacation during pandemic? Are there good things to do and great restaurants to dine in?* My answer is definitely *"Yes."*

However, traveling during the pandemic has its pros and cons and we'll address those here.

I like what Candy Aluli of Maui Accommodations wrote when asked if it is safe to visit Maui right now: Her answer is "Yes!" and continues with the explanation:

The state of Hawaii has been very successful in controlling the virus, and we have one of the lowest COVID-19 mortality rates in the U.S. Maui is one of the safest destinations in the world.... We have worked hard and sacrificed to make it that way.

The tourism shutdown created a great deal of suffering here—Maui has the highest unemployment rate in the state, and at one point we had the highest unemployment rate in the United States. So, these past months have not been easy for us. But our residents are committed to keeping our community safe by wearing masks, social distancing, and following other recommended guidelines. At this time, we have only an occasional new positive case of COVID-19 on the island of Maui. Keeping everyone on our island—both residents and visitors—safe and healthy is our top priority.

Good to Read: <u>Visiting Maui During COVID-19: What You Need To Know</u>

https://www.mauiaccommodations.com/blog/visiting-maui-during-covid-what-you-need-to-know/

Aside from considering COVID-19 restrictions, I understand that making a decision on when to come to Maui will also be based on various circumstances such as vacation from school and work, airline and hotel rates (high season is more expensive than off season), weather and local happenings.

Here are some things to consider when deciding the best time for you to visit Maui.

The busiest time to visit Maui is around the holidays – Thanksgiving, Christmas, New Year and Easter. During these times, traffic is heavier, and airfare and hotel accommodation rates are high. We call it the "high season" in tourism. Despite the high rates, it is a wonderful time to visit because it is a festive season, with lights and decorations. It is also the whale season. December to April is the best time for nature lovers to visit Maui.

If you are on a budget, the best time to come is Spring and Fall. Travel and accommodation prices are the lowest in these two "shoulder seasons."

Maui does not have the distinctive four seasons because we do not have snow. Many travel books will say we have two seasons: summer, from May to October and winter, from November to April.

Let us discuss the pros and cons of coming to Maui based on the four seasons that are experienced on the mainland.

Winter (December to early March)

There are more chances of rain in winter on Maui than any other time of the year. However, it rains infrequently on the West and South sides of Maui, even in the winter.

It is also more expensive due to the holidays. However, if you live in a snowy area, it is a great time to escape to Maui to get out of snow.

For surfers, the biggest waves happen in December. Surfing contests occur then.

And the most popular reason to come to Maui in winter is the "whales"! Whales swim down from Alaska, are back on Maui, usually begin appearing in December, and it peak from January to March.

Spring (late March – April)

There are still more chances of rain in spring compared to summer. However, rates are generally lower on airfare and accommodations. Plumerias are starting to bloom. The crowds are smaller because many are still in school.

Plumerias on Maui

Summer (May to September)

This is the hottest time of the year, but for many visitors that is often what they want. Most of the students are out of school for vacation so the island tends to be busy. You can do more during the day because days are longer during summer, with the least chances of rain (possibly no rain at all during your visit).

Fall (October to November)

There might be a little spike in visits on the week of Thanksgiving but weeks prior and weeks after are the slowest of the year, thus we call it "the low season." Plan to experience beautiful dramatic sunsets and wonderful weather.

PERSONAL NOTES AND PLANNING

CHAPTER 2

WHERE, OH WHERE, TO STAY ON MAUI?

Deciding where to stay on Maui depends on your budget, what you want to do and what type of weather you enjoy. Let's start with understanding the lay of the land, how regions are divided, where the towns are, the general weather in these towns and the amenities each town offers.

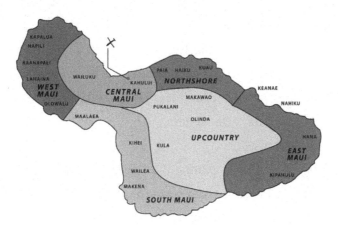

There are two major resort areas on Maui – one the Westside of the island (Lahaina/Kaanapali side) and the other one on the Southside (Kihei/Wailea). Most likely, when you are planning a vacation (*especially if it is your first time*), you choose to stay in one of these two areas.

West Maui

West Maui includes the town of **Lahaina, Kaanapali, Honokawai, Napili, Kahana and Kapalua.** The west side is the "more touristy" side of Maui. You will like this side of the island if you enjoy great hotels, restaurants, activities, shopping and beaches – all with easy access for the first-time visitors.

My friend Jon Blum of www.MauiHawaii.org prefers the west side, specifically Kaanapali. According to him, it is more beautiful (lush green mountains) and it is very close to Lahaina (fun historic tourist town and boat harbor). Lahaina is a place for boat tours, shopping and luaus. West Maui also has the most beautiful golf courses.

The Hyatt Regency Maui Resort and Spa, The Westin Maui Hotel, Sheraton Maui Resort and Spa, Montage Kapalua Bay, Kaanapali Beach Hotel, Royal Lahaina Resort and Ritz Carlton Kapalua are some of the big chain hotels here. Kaanapali Beach Hotel and Royal Lahaina are less expensive (and less luxurious), but they are famous for their "Hawaiiana" atmosphere.

Kaanapali was the first planned destination resort on Maui. Just a few miles up the road from Lahaina, this resort has a beautiful pristine beach, some great spots for snorkeling, a shopping center

(Whaler's Village) and in the center of the resort lies the green expanse of Kaanapali Golf Course. The Hyatt Regency, Westin, Sheraton, and Kaanapali Beach are major hotels in this area built next to the golf course. Black Rock is a famous landmark for swimming and jumping at the Sheraton Hotel. This is where this book's cover photo was taken.

There are also many beachfront condominiums for rent such as Westin Kaanapali Ocean Resort, Maui Kaanapali Villas, Kaanapali Ocean Inn, Maui Eldorado, Kaanapali Royal and Kaanapali Alii. If you are visiting Maui for the first time, staying in the Kaanapali area is very convenient because of all the activities, shops and restaurants are situated along the entire coastline.

Napili is the gateway to Kapalua, located 9 miles north of Lahaina. There are timeshares and condos available such as Napili Beach Resort and Napili Village. It is a popular place in the Westside to walk and jog, and also for snorkeling, surfing and scuba diving in Napili Bay.

Kapalua is situated on a nature preserve. This world-class destination has pristine beaches and three world-class championship golf courses. My friend Sheila Beal, the owner of the famous website GoVisitHawaii.com, said that Kapalua is among her favorite places to stay on Maui. The luxury hotel Ritz Carlton is in Kapalua.

South Maui

South Maui is the Sunshine region. The towns included on South Maui are Maalaea, Kihei, Wailea and Makena. The major resort area is in Wailea. Though it may be the hottest and driest, it is also the most popular coastline on Maui for "sun lovers." This part of the island has the least rain throughout the year. This region is not as touristy as the resort area on West Maui but it still can get crowded in "high season" (November to March).

Wailea contains the major luxury hotels such as Grand Wailea, Four Seasons, Andaz, Fairmont Kea Lani and Wailea Beach Marriott. All these hotels are top notch in the industry and you can't go wrong with any of them.

There are also many luxury condos and villas to choose from such as the oceanfront condos Wailea Beach Villas and Wailea Elua.

Kihei is less expensive and has a wide selection of budget condo rentals. Kihei condos are still walking distance from the beach and many are oceanfront. Paul Brodie, the author of Maui – *Ten Ways to Enjoy the Best Food, Beaches and Location While on Vacation* says Kihei is his favorite town. He thinks Kihei has better value in terms of price and many of the locals live in the area. For him, it feels like home. It is more like a traditional town and has great beaches and restaurants.

Some of the popular condominium complexes to stay are Kamaole Sands, Maui Kamaole, Kihei Surfside, Royal Mauian, Koa Lagoon, Luana Kai Resort.

Makena, the farthest town south, is the least crowded and least developed part of South Maui. The "Makena Beach and Golf Resort" closed down and is now being rebuilt as a more luxurious and exclusive Makena Beach Club (completion date to be determined). There are however some luxury condos available for rent. Check out Makena Surf condos on VRBO and Airbnb. Makena is where the pristine Makena Beach, divides into "Big Beach" and "Little Beach."

Maalaea is the oceanfront village close to the West Maui Border. It is windy in this part of the island. All the wind from the Pacific funnels between the West Maui Mountains and Haleakala and comes out in Maalaea. Here you can rent many oceanfront condos at affordable prices. Some boat tours leave from the Maalaea Marina, which is more convenient for those staying in the south side, so you don't need to go to Lahaina for all boating activities.

Now that we've discussed the two regions where the major resort areas are, let us take a look at the other regions: Central, Upcountry, North Shore and East Maui.

Central Maui

Central Maui towns include **Kahului, Waikapu and Wailuku.** The airport where you will land, OGG, is located in Kahului.

Kahului is the commercial town of Maui. This is where you will find Costco, Walmart and Target. It is also where Queen Kaahumanu Mall is located. Aside from the commercial centers, there are also many local residential neighborhoods in this town. This was known as the "Dream City" to thousands of former sugar-cane workers.

The Courtyard by Marriott is a relatively new hotel in Kahului near the airport. If your flight is arriving late or if you are leaving very early on the morning, this is a good option. Also ideal for a short business trip but not for a family vacation. They have a complimentary airport shuttle.

Wailuku is the "Historic Town" and also where most of the State and County offices are. On Main Street, Wailuku has many local shops such as Native Intelligence. A popular (and historical) place to stay is the Old Wailuku Inn at Ulupono. There is also the new vacation rental called The Blue Door on Church Street. The famous landmark, the Iao Valley, is located in Wailuku.

Waikapu is the location of Maui Tropical Plantation and Kumu Farms. Another famous landmark in Waikapu is the King Kamehameha

Golf Club. This is also where the now famous Sunflowers on Maui first happened. Pacific Biodiesel owns a field in Waikapu where they plant sunflowers to produce biodiesel. When the first batch of sunflowers bloomed in 2018 Maui residents (and visitors alike) were so excited! You most likely have seen many photos of sunflowers on Maui in your Instagram that year).

Waikapu is a residential area – there are no hotels or inns to stay although there might be some random room for rent in Airbnb.

Upcountry Maui

Upcountry towns **Pukalani, Haliimaile, Makawao** and **Kula** are away from the beach, up on the Haleakala mountain, with cooler temperatures and green fields. Upcountry is the part of Maui on the valley side of Haleakala.

Makawao is a small paniolo town (Hawaiian Cowboy). My mother-in-law loved visiting this small town. You can stroll through some of the best gift shops and small galleries highlighting Maui's talented local artists.

Pukalani, Haliimaile, and Kula – I lumped these towns together – mostly residential but for those who desire a cooler climate and do not care if they are far from the beach, these towns are great. There are many great activities to do here especially in Kula where the Ulupalakua Winery, Alii Kula Lavender Farm, and the Haleakala National Park are located. You will be able to find a few Bed and Breakfast places via Airbnb and VRBO. For romantic upcountry cottages with beautiful panoramic views, check out Kula Lodge.

North Shore

Paia has become a destination in its own right. Paia is a small town with big character and personality. So far it has managed to avoid becoming touristy or gentrified, and it is still largely populated by a diverse mix of colorful and eccentric people – lovers of art, surfers, vegans, who are drawn to the independent bohemian vibe. The town is filled with quaint shops, cafes, and restaurants. Paia Bay and Baldwin Beach is also close, as is Hookipa. A popular place to stay is Paia Inn but there are other Bed and Breakfasts in the area as well. Mana Food is a "go to place" grocery store for healthy food in this part of town.

Haiku and Huelo – Mostly residential. Like Paia, these towns also have an eclectic vibe. Sometimes they are known as the Hippie Town, with inexpensive places to rent via Airbnb and VRBO. You can also stay at the more luxurious Mama's Fish House Inn near Hookipa Beach. Mama's Fish House is the best restaurant on Maui, and maybe in the world. It is currently number 1 on Open Table in the world. It is expensive but worth the high cost. The oceanfront location, ambiance, fresh fish and ingredients, delicious cuisine, it is a true Hawaiian dining experience. Haiku Marketplace at the Haiku Cannery is the hub of Haiku Community. In addition, there is also the Pauwela Cannery.

East Maui

Keanae, Hana, Kipahulu – When talking about places to stay on the East Side of Maui, Hana Maui Resort is on the top of my mind. Yes, you can find various bed and breakfast places to rent if you are on a budget, but for honeymooners and for individuals who want to experience convenience and serenity, I recommend spending the extra bucks and staying at Hana Maui Resort. I have stayed at this place four times already and enjoyed each and every "staycation" there. (It was initially Hotel Hana, then became Travaasa Hana, and now Hana Maui Resort by Hyatt Hotels).

Most of the VACATION RENTAL CONDOS are also now accepting booking. You can check AirBnB and VRBO. There are also local agencies you can check for list of vacations rentals such as MauiAccomodations.com and RentalsMaui.com. Often, you can save money by going directly through the local property owners and managers.

PERSONAL NOTES AND PLANNING

CHAPTER 3

DO I REALLY NEED TO TAKE THAT TEST BEFORE I GO?

Pre-Travel, Arrival and Transportation

When planning a vacation on Maui, you have to have three choices:

1) You can opt to quarantine for 10 days and not worry about following in detail the Safe Travel Program for by-passing the quarantine

2) You decide to abide by the **Safe Travel Program to bypass the 10 day quarantine** via Pre-travel testing.

3) You decide to get vaccinated and skip the testing requirement. (July 2021 update)

Most people will choose #2 or #3. In this chapter we will discuss choice #2 extensively (as of writing this book, these requirements are still in place). However, make sure you read the June 2021 Update at the end of this chapter, because by the time you are reading this book, the Hawaii Safe Travels Program might not be applicable any longer.

> *Make sure to read the "June 2021 Update" at the end of this Chapter and also the "Final Thoughts and Update" at the end of the book.*

Important Safe Travel Program You MUST Know and Follow

Arrival on Maui during COVID-19 Pandemic and beyond is now more complicated than Pre-COVID-19. There are IMPORTANT things that you need to know and do, that you didn't have to do before. Example is the "Safe Travel Program".

> OFFICIAL WEBSITE TO CHECK OFTEN FOR UPDATES WHEN PLANNING TO VIST: https://hawaii-covid19.com/ and particularly this section: https://hawaiicovid19.com/travel/

Safe Travel Program

- **Go to travel.hawaii.gov and create a "Safe Travels Account."** This is the mandatory State of Hawaii Travel & Health Form. Everyone who is traveling to Hawaii must fill out this form whether you are requesting quarantine or not.
- **Do not be intimidated by this process.** I know that for millennials, these steps are easy because they are used to digital systems. However, for some Baby Boomers and older people, this many seem overwhelming. I want to assure you that you can do this easily.

- One tip I have is to **use a desktop or laptop instead of doing this on your phone or Ipad** when setting up this account. And yes, seek assistance from those who are digitally savvy family and friends - could be your children, grandchildren or family friends.

Let us look the basics as we go through the process in bullet points (based on the video they show you at travel.hawaii.gov)

- The State of Hawaii has a mandatory 10 day quarantine and passenger verification process for traveling to the islands.
- Beginning December 17, 2020, passengers who test negative for COVID19 in a pre-travel test, taken within 72 hours of departure, will not be subject to the State's 10 Day quarantine program. (For Maui, an additional requirement to download An Aloha Safe App (see July update page 23 & 24)

VERY IMPORTANT: Covid19 tests will only be accepted from State of Hawaii's trusted partners. The current list of trusted partners can be found at https://hawaiicovid19.com/travel-partners

HERE ARE THE 7 EASY STEPS TO FOLLOW:

1. Sign up to create a use account. Each traveling adult must create their own account.

Go to https://travel.hawaii.gov

- The first page you will see on that website has a simple form for you to fill out and a video for you to watch and learn of the process.

- The form will consist of two fields to fill out: 1) email address and 2) password.
- Once you submit that, watch the video, then check your email (the one you submitted in the form)
- By this time, you should have received an email confirmation. The email will be from "Travel" (travel@notifyhawaii.gov)
- Once you clicked the link in that email, you will receive another email notifying you that your email had been verified.
- Go back to travel.hawaii.gov and log in with your verified email and password.
- You will be taken to another form to fill -out. This time it is more than just email and password.
- When you are filling this out on a desktop or laptop (as I suggested), remember to have your phone next to you because there is an item on the form that requires phone number verification.

2. Once the account is created, enter your trip details.

- Make sure to **add trip for each leg of travel**. A QR code will be needed for each leg of your trip.

3. Upload your documents:

- **First, your COVID-19 results (or vaccination card).** You are only able to upload a COVID-19 test result taken within 72 hours from final leg of travel.
- If and when your test result is verified, the status of the document will show Covid19 Negative.

- Don't forget to upload a recent picture of yourself (selfies are ok). This is voluntary but highly recommended.
- Then wait. **The questionnaire will be available to you 24 hours before your departure.**

4. Twenty-Four (24) hours before your departure, log in to your user account and complete the Travel Health Questionnaire.

Here are the questions in which you will have to answer "yes" or "no":

Do you feel ill now?
Have you had a flu vaccine?
Have you taken a medicine (example Tylenol or Ibuprofen) in the last 24 hours to bring your fever down?
Have you signed a 10 day quarantine order that is currently in effect?
Have you traveled outside the State of Hawaii (other than your home state, if not a Hawaii resident) in the last 14 days?

5. Submit the completed questionnaire and you will receive your QR code.

- Use your phone to get the QR code. This will speed up your process in the airport.
- I suggest screenshotting and also printing on paper to be safe. The screen shot and paper copy will come in handy when the power or internet at the airport is sporadic.
- Remember, your 10 day quarantine begins on the day you enter the State if you did not participate in the pre-travel testing program (effective December 17, 2020). Your daily check-ins begin the day after you arrive.

6. Download the AlohaSafe Alert App on your mobile phone.
Failure to do so will result in a mandatory 10-day quarantine period.

Exceptions to the Maui contact tracing requirements.

There are a few situations, as per the emergency rule quoted above, that will not require the AlohaSafe Alert app. The exceptions are:

- Traveler utilizes an alternative contact tracing app. (must be a Google-Apple Exposure Notification System).
- Any travelers under the age of 18.
- Any traveler who does not possess a mobile device, when at least one other person in the party has the app.

7. Proceed through the airport checkpoint.

Note: Some airlines (Alaska, Hawaiian and United) have organized a Pre-Clear option which will help you save time and help avoid additional document screening upon arrival. Check with your airlines if they have a Pre-clear program.

If pre-screen was not an option for you, have the following items ready upon arrival:

#1 **Your QR Code** must be readily available on your mobile device or printed in paper.

#2 Have a **valid government issued ID** for each traveling adult. (Example: Driver's License)

#3. Bring your **cell phones charged and working properly.** Your contact information will be verified at the check point.

#4. If you have quarantine exemption, please bring your letter or evidence of the exemption with you.

#5. Be sure to **bring your test results to the airport** with you for screening process for all status results in uploaded documents.

Once you are screened at the airport, your trip details will be updated with your Safe Travels Exemption Information.

You will be able to show it to your ground transportation and hotel accommodations as evidence that you are exempt from the mandatory 10 day quarantine.

It can be accessed under "Trips".

For more information, plan to go to:

https://hawaiicovid19.com/travel

June/July 2021
Hawaii Safe Travel Update

As of June 15, 2021, all inter-county (inter-island) travel restrictions were dropped.

As of June 15, all travelers fully vaccinated (plus two weeks) within Hawaii are now able to travel via trans-Pacific routes without a pre-travel test. Travelers entering the state of Hawaii (traveling from US mainland and Alaska) who had been vaccinated in Hawaii (at least one shot done in Hawaii) may bypass the quarantine with-out a pre-travel test.

Beginning July 8, 2021, individuals fully vaccinated in the United States may enter the Hawaii without pre-travel testing/quarantine starting the 15th day after the completion of their vaccination. The vaccination record document must be uploaded onto Safe Travels and printed out prior to departure and the traveler must have a hard copy in hand when arriving in Hawaii.

When Hawaii reaches 70% of vaccination rate, the Safe Travels Program may be able to conclude. This means the Safe Travels Program requirements mentioned in Chapter 3 of this book will not be needed.

Make sure you read the updated requirements at www.hawaii-covid19.com

Car Rental and Transportation

Do you need to rent a car during your Maui Vacation? The answer is "yes." It is highly recommended. Renting is car is the best way to travel around the island of Maui. There are other options such as Uber, Lyft, Shuttle Service, Maui Bus System, and Travel Tour, but those are all limited. Rent a car for convenience to fully enjoy your Maui Vacation.

Reserve a car prior to your arrival on Maui especially during high season. Then you can pick up at the airport when you arrive. **When you pick up your rental car, you have to show your Safe Travel QR Code to verify you are not required to quarantine.**

There are a number of large car rental companies operating with the airport such as Alamo, Avis, Budget, Dollars, Enterprise, Hertz and National. However, there are also many locally operated, such as Kimo's Rent a Car, Kihei Rent a Car and Discount Hawaii Car Rental.

June 2021 Update:

Booking a rental car on Maui has become a costly part of the Maui vacation in 2021 due to shortage. Some car agencies charging as much as $400 per day during the surge of visitor in Spring. Make sure you have car reservations taken cared of at the same time you book your accommodation and flight.

Additional Insight on this blog post at A Maui Blog: **https:// amauiblog.com/how-to-navigate-the-maui-rental-car -shortage-and-enjoy-your-hawaiian-vacation/**

More information on Hawaii Tourism Authority website: **https://www.hawaiitourismauthority.org/Covid-19-updates/ ground-transportation/Maui-transportation-options/**

PERSONAL NOTES AND PLANNING

CHAPTER 4

LET'S GO SHOPPING ON MAUI

Grocery Shopping

So you've arrived on Maui, you've gone through the Safe Travel Process, you got your luggage picked up, you have secured a rental car, and you are on your way to the hotel or condo…

For those of you staying in a hotel, chances are you won't need or want to stop by a grocery store. You just want to go straight to your hotel and relax, or maybe change and go straight to the pool or beach after (depending on what time you arrived).

If you are staying in a condo and would like to hire a grocery delivery service prior to your arrival, you may call Maui Grocery service at 808-280-7526. They can stock your pantry and refrigerator with what you need.

For those of you staying in a condo but didn't want to hire grocery shopping services, you probably will want to stop by a grocery store to buy some basic needs.

Most travel guidebooks recommend stopping by **Costco** to get your groceries because it is close to the airport. No wonder Costco in Maui is one of the top sellers among all the Costco in the world. The prices are cheaper than the regular grocery stores but many of the items require you to buy in bulk. It really depends on the size of your group and the length of your stay. When you are coming to visit as a family and staying at a condo, you will probably save a lot of money by doing this. You can buy your milk, bread, wine, and even some meat for barbecue. They also have prepared dinner and other food items.

If there is only one or two of you, it is probably better to stop by the new Safeway in Kahului (also close to the airport) or go to Target or Walmart.

If you decide to stop by a grocery store from the airport, one thing I recommend is to have someone stay in the car (or van). Read more about this on Chapter 7 Safety Reminders.

Aside from Costco, other places to shops for groceries are Target, Walmart, Safeway, Foodland and Times Supermarket.

For natural food stores, you can go to Whole Foods (Kahului), Alive and Well (Kahului), Mana Foods (Paia) and Hawaiian Moons (Kihei).

A gentle reminder and encouragement: Buy local as much as you can. You can get fresh produce and you will also be helping our farmers and local entrepreneurs. I highly recommend going to farmers market. The next section is about Farmers Market and Swap Meet.

Farmers Market and Swap Meet

One of the best shopping experiences is going to a Farmers Market, especially when buying fresh fruit, vegetables and produce.

Buy local and buy fresh. It is also a great opportunity for you to meet local farmers and artisans and get to know Maui people more.

Kahului Swap Meet – Before COVID-19, the most recommended place to go was the Kahului Swap Meet, also known as the **Maui Swap Meet**. Its central at the UH Maui College Campus location made it easy to visit.

This famous Maui Swap Meet at the UH Maui College area closed due to COVID-19. **The good news: they re-opened just before I published this book! – (reopened June 12, 2021)**

While the Maui Swap Meet was closed, a **new Kahului Swap Meet happens at the Maui Market** Place Parking Lot on Dairy Road, every Saturday 8am to 2pm. No charge. With temperature checks, hand sanitizers provided, mask is required and stores are arranged for proper social distancing. There are not as many vendors as the former Kahului Swap Meet but participation is evolving.

Here are a few more Farmers Markets that are open:

Upcountry Farmers Market – This is one of the oldest and most popular farmers market on Maui. It is located at Kula Malu Town Center next to Longs Drugs in Pukalani. It is open on Saturdays, 7am to 11 am. Enjoy a beautiful early morning Upcountry with local produce from variety of farms and locally made products. Phone: 808-283-3257.

Napili Farmers Market – This is a popular and well-loved farmers market on the Westside. It is located at 4900 Honoapiilani Hwy (corner of Honoapiilani Hwy & Napilihau St. in Lahaina). Open Wednesdays and Saturday 8am to 12 noon. Fresh Maui produce; local organically managed produce and other local products such as honey, fresh juices, kombucha and more. Vegan friendly. Phone 808-663-5060

Maui Fresh Farmers Market – Located at Queen Kaahumanu Mall at the center court. Open on Tuesdays, Wednesdays, and Fridays, 8am to 12 noon. They have local farm produce, gourmet food, plants, and flowers. Phone 808-298-4289

Farmers Market Kihei – Located on North Kihei next to the ABC Store, Ululani Shave Ice and Sugar Beach Bake Shop. Open Monday to Thursday 8am to 4pm and Friday am to 5pm. It's a locally owned fruit and vegetable stand with fresh baked goods, dips, and salsas. They also offer acai bowls, breakfast bagels and smoothies.

Farmers Market at KukuiMall in Kihei – An additional Farmers Market in Kihei happens on Saturday morning 8am to 12 noon at the parking lot behind Kukui Mall.

Kumu Farms – Known for their delicious GMO Free papayas, Kumu Farms ins located at the entrance of Maui Tropical Plantation. Although the Maui Tropical Plantation closed down during pandemic, Kumu Farms remain open. They also do CSA boxes and they ship gift boxes of papaya and Pineapple to the mainland. Open Tuesday to Saturday 9am to 4pm. Phone: 808-244-4800.

Laakea Village – This is a unique farmers market run by the non-profit organization with the same name Laakea Village. Laakea Village empowers people of all abilities to live, work, learn, play and thrive together to live their greatest potential. Located at 639 Baldwin Ave. in Paia, open Monday to Friday 11 am to 4:30 pm. Phone 808-579-8398

Farmers Market at Lahaina Jodo Mission – This is a new farmers market. They had a very successful opening and it is thriving. Open on 2nd and 4th Thursday of the month, 4pm to 7pm.

Farmers Market at Oskie Rice Arena in Kula – **Wednesday** 9am to 1pm, **Saturday** from 12 noon until 4pm.

New: Wailea Village Farmers Market – On January 26, 2021 Wailea Village launched a weekly farmer's market in its courtyard. It is open from 8 a.m. to 12 p.m. every Tuesday. This is in addition to their once-a-month Wailea Sunset Market that happens every first Thursday of the month.

Internet Resource: edible Hawaiian Farm Guide https://ediblehi.com/8th-annual-hawaii-farm-guide-spring-2021/

Clothing and Souvenir Shopping

For those of you who enjoy shopping while on vacation, there are plenty of malls and local shops.

On the West side you'll find the Whalers Village, The Outlets in Lahaina, Lahaina Gateway Store and more. You can also find many Mom and Pop and locally owned shops on Front Street. One of my favorite boutiques is Maui Memories located at The Pioneer Inn.

On the South Side are The Shops at Wailea, Wailea Village, Kamaole Shopping Center, Rainbow Mall, Dolphin Plaza, Azeka's and more. Two of my favorite local stores at Sunkissed Wahine (located at Kalama Village in Kihei) and Tutu's Pantry (located at Rainbow Mall in Kihei)

As I mentioned earlier, there are also many wonderful local shops in Paia and Makawao town.

PERSONAL NOTES AND PLANNING

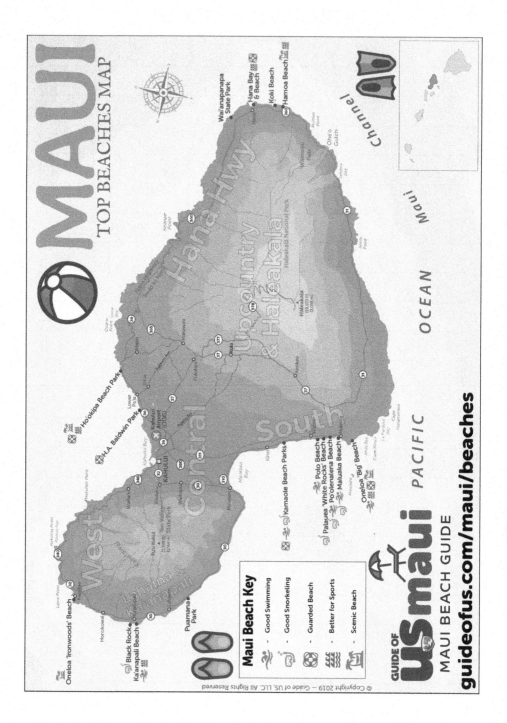

MAUI
TOP BEACHES MAP

Maui Channel

PACIFIC OCEAN

Waianapanapa State Park
Hana Bay & Beach
Koki Beach
Hamoa Beach

Hana Hwy

Upcountry & Haleakala
Haleakala National Park
Haleakala (10,023 m) (3,055 m)

Central

West

Lahaina & Kaanapali

South

Hookipa Beach Park
Lower Paia
H.A. Baldwin Park
Kahului Airport (OGG)
KAHULUI

Oneloa 'Ironwoods' Beach
Black Rock
Kaanapali Beach
Horokawai

Puamana Park

Kamaole Beach Parks
Polo Beach
Palauea 'White Rocks' Beach
Po'olenalena Beach
Maluaka Beach
Oneloa 'Big' Beach

Maui Beach Key

- 🏄 - Good Swimming
- 🤿 - Good Snorkeling
- 🛟 - Guarded Beach
- 〰 - Better for Sports
- 🏞 - Scenic Beach

GUIDE OF
USmaui
MAUI BEACH GUIDE
guideofus.com/maui/beaches

CHAPTER 5

SO MUCH TO DO, SO LITTLE TIME!

This chapter is hard to write because there are so many things to do on Maui. This is not a comprehensive list. What I will share with more details are the activities that I personally recommend you can do while visiting, and also the top activities to do with or without the pandemic.

Go to the Beach and Enjoy the Ocean

Going to the beach is the best activity you can do on Maui in 2021 and beyond. When Maui was "closed," many of the beaches were empty, and nature had its rest. When we had the "stay at home" order, the beaches had time to "heal." Now that Maui has opened up, there are more people at the beach, but still not as many as in previous years. There's never been a better time to visit the beaches on Maui.

There are many ways you can enjoy the beach and ocean on Maui. For those who truly just want to relax on their Maui vacation, bringing a beach chair and umbrella and lounging on the shore is great. Most rental condos include these for your use. Bring a book (or listen to an audio book) and occasionally take a dip in the water.

For those who are more active, there are many water activities and water sports to do:

- surfing
- boogie boarding
- stand up paddling
- canoe paddling
- windsurfing
- kite boarding
- snorkeling
- scuba diving
- snuba diving
- and the latest craze on Maui is foiling.

Foiling is a hybrid of surfing and hydrofoil technology, foil surfing replaces the traditional fin at the bottom of a surfboard with a much longer, hydrodynamically designed fin called a blade. That blade is longer than the fin on an average surfboard and has wings at its base.

I highly recommend trying at least one of the water sports when you are on Maui. Maybe take up a basic surfing lesson if you don't know how to surf. There are many activity tours that can assist you with this, Maui Wave Riders (www.mauiwaveriders.com) and Hawaiian Paddle Sports (hawaiipaddlesports.com) among them.

The important thing to do is to make a list of what you want to do or experience at the beach. You can't do them all, so choose whatever makes you happy.

My favorite thing to do is walk the beach at the end of the day and watch the sunset. I never get tired of doing these two leisurely activities. I live close to Kamaole Beach III so I walk to there from my house and regularly enjoy the Maui sunset at the beach.

So, what are the best beaches on Maui? I can tell you what I think the Top Beaches on Maui are, but the truth is, the best beaches on Maui for your vacation depends on you. Usually, it is the closest beach to where you are staying, so when you are planning on where to stay on Maui, check out the beaches that are near. I know surfers who like to surf at Hookipa would rent a vacation rental place in Haiku so they can surf on Hookipa regularly. Families who come and stay in some of the Napili condos love Napili Bay. If you enjoy lounging, then Wailea Beach or Kaanapali Beach would be great for you.

If you are a first-time visitor and would like more information, here are some the Best Beaches on Maui. Take some time to visit some of them in addition to the beach close to where you are staying.

Best Beaches on Maui

There are many great beaches on Maui, and here are some of my picks. This section on Best Beaches on Maui (in italics) is written by Mark Goldberg, owner of www.MauiGuidebook.com. **If you want a detailed information on Maui beaches, with maps and reviews, go to www.mauiguidebook.com**

West Maui Beaches:

Kaanapali Beach – *A mile-long, spectacularly perfect beach that is home to seven resorts, high-end shopping, various restaurants and activities. Kaanapali Beach runs from Black Rock to Canoe Beach, fronted by seven resorts, Whalers Village Mall, and many fine shops & restaurants. The beach itself is perfection. Long, wide and sandy, the water entry and swimming are glorious. Black Rock offers cliff jumping (and cliff-jumper watching.) There are activities galore. There is also a long concrete walk that you can stroll along as you meander between shops, eats, drinks, sunset, and the beach.*

Honolua Bay *is a spectacular place to snorkel or dive, if you know where to go. Beach uses are mediocre. Honolua Bay is part of a Marine Life Conservation District, so there is no fishing (or taking of any natural resources, including marine life and even rocks.) The primary draw here today is snorkeling and surfing;*

Napili Bay – *A less crowded, low-key resort beach with a much more family feel than many in West Maui. Napili Bay has a sandy cove nestled in mid-range resort which is itself nestled in a residential neighborhood. Entry is sandy, and the bottom is sandy with moderately steep entry and then reef further out (you can see the reef in the Google Satellite Image below). Sea turtles frequent the bay, and snorkeling can be fair when the surf is mellow. When the surf is up visibility, and thus snorkeling, is poor.*

Baby Beach *in Lahaina is mostly visited by local families with young children. The beach is protected by an exposed stretch of reef, creating a calm shallow area where small children won't be knocked down by a big wave,* *though even here they of course need adult supervision. Baby Beach is in the north part of Lahaina near the Lahaina Jodo Mission.*

Kapalua Beach – *Situated in a very protected cove, this cove is virtually a large swimming pool. Fair snorkeling, as visibility is frequently not the best. Beach is backed by development and there is a fair amount of rocky bottom in the cove.*

South Maui Beaches:

Keawakapu Beach – *A much loved long sandy beach at the end of South Kihei Road. It is a less crowded beach where Kihei meets Wailea. The shoreline is fully developed here, including impressive beach houses, condos and a couple of restaurants. Much of the development has been kept a tasteful distance from the beach – keeping the majority distinctly separate; the beach refreshingly non-commercialized.*

Kamaole Beach I, II and III – *Kamaole is a very popular set of beaches for locals and visitors. Beautiful, long, 1.5 mile sandy beaches with incredible views of Molokini, Kaho'olawe and Lana'i islands. Kam III has one of the most regular South Maui shore breaks for boogie-boarding. Snorkeling opportunities are plentiful. Full facilities and family friendly.*

Wailea Beach – *Consistently rated one of the world's best beaches. Crowded with resort guests and their accouterments. Wailea Beach is unquestionably a study in beach perfection, and if you don't mind a resort vibe (and a crowd to go with it) this is a truly outstanding beach.*

The beach is wide, the sand perfect, and the ocean inviting. Views of Kahoolawe, Molokini, Lanai and the sights (and sounds) of whales are common in winter.

Ulua Beach – *Good swimming, boogie boarding and excellent beginner to intermediate snorkeling around the rocky outcrop on the north end of the beach. Ulua Beach fronts the Wailea Elua Village condos and is popular with dive instructors, as there is a good beginner level dive at the outer reef.*

Mokapu Beach – *Quarter-mile long pocket of sandy beach fronting the Andaz Wailea Hotel. Good swimming, boogie boarding and excellent snorkeling around the rocky outcrop to the south.*

Makena Beach – *(Big Beach and Little Beach) -* **Big Beach** *is a beautiful, long, wide, undeveloped sandy beach. Impressive, with huge views and a large shore-break. Big Beach is a must-see. A wicked shore-break exists here when the surf is up that can be dangerous for the inexperienced.* **Little Beach** *is this nook of a beach just north of Big Beach. It is commonly known as the "nude beach" on Maui, although that is not official. It is illegal to be nude on the beaches in Hawaii. Little beach can get crowded as some visitors have this on their "bucket list".*

Cove Park – *Cove Park is the best place to learn to surf in South Maui. It is also a wonderful beach of convenience for the local condos and residents. Just at the south point of Kalama Park. Most commonly used for beginner surf lessons, many instructors are set up ready to go every day of the week. There is a hidden cove right next door that is better for swimming and beach (see kayak video below) The park is primarily go-to for most visitors for surf lessons. Full facilities at Kalama Park immediately adjacent.*

Kalepolepo Beach *is a historically significant Hawaiian fishpond and a quiet beach for those staying in the area. The beach here is small, and uncrowded. With a dozen beaches that are the definition of perfection just minutes away, few visitors from the resorts further south will wind up coming here. From that perspective, this is more in the class of a "convenience beach" left for residents and visitors staying in the area (yeah, we're that spoiled here!)*

Central Maui Beaches:

Kanaha Beach *is a very popular beach for locals and watersports enthusiasts. Beautiful, long, two-mile sandy beach with incredible views of the West Maui Mountains. Among the best kiteboarding and windsurfing on Planet Earth.*

North Shore Beaches:

Baby Beach in Paia *– A beautiful beach and protected lagoon just before Paia on the North Shore of Maui. An exposed stretch of reef, connected to a rocky red-dirt point on the west end of the beach creates a calm lagoon protected from the ocean. This lagoon is perfect for young children and parents. It is also a great place to swim laps, explore, or just and hang out on the beach soaking in the scenery.*

Hookipa Beach *– A world-renowned windsurfing destination with often dramatic and impressive surf for sightseers as well. Hookipa is Mecca to the windsurfing world (and no slouch for board surfing, either.) There are professional windsurfing competitions held here, and on just about any day with wind (most) you can watch pros doing their thing. Hookipa also* *provides sightseers a stunning backdrop to watch the best effortlessly play with the ocean in a way that mere mortals can only dream of.*

If you're considering getting in to surf or sail here, you'd better be skilled enough for the conditions – especially if the orange flags are out and the surf is big. Even on smaller to average days, sudden and quickly building afternoon winds, strong rip currents and shallow reef can quickly take control from overoptimistic novices. The inexperienced would also be well advised to study the ocean and locally experienced surfers carefully before entering. If you don't see the best way in and out ask the guards how to avoid the rip (and then the reef) when you come back in.

Baldwin Beach – *A beautiful, long white-sand beach on Maui's North Shore. A favorite with local families.*

Baldwin Beach is a wonderful, long, wide, sandy beach park just outside of Paia. Fully equipped with lifeguards, bathrooms, showers, barbecues, picnic tables and a covered pavilion.

Paia Bay *is a favorite for bodyboarders and bodysurfers. The break is generally just a bit off shore and overhead, so fins are a good idea. Definitely not a place to bodyboard unless you have experience as the waves can get large. There is another break for surfers further off shore.*

In the winter the surf here can get huge, and dangerous rip currents can form. If it looks really rough, even though you'll probably see locals boogie boarding, don't go in unless you're very experienced.

East Maui Beaches:

Hamoa Beach – *This beach is often ranked up there with the famous beaches in the resort areas of Maui, and deservingly so. A postcard-perfect 100? wide by 1000? long crescent. Hamoa Beach is surrounded by cliffs, with two points of public access – stairs leading down from the hotel shuttle dropoff and a small service road at the other end. (walk, don't drive on this). Hamoa Beach is also a popular surf break – in fact this break has been surfed by Hawaiians since ancient times. Boogie boarding and bodysurfing are also popular here. Snorkeling can be good around the left of the cove, however this beach is exposed to open ocean; be aware that powerful currents and surf can often be present – especially toward the ends of the beach.*

Wainapanapa Black Sand Beach – *Spectacular views of rugged shoreline, sea arches, black sand beach, and more. Swimming is often marginal. Simply stated, Waianapanapa State Park is among the very best of the Road to Hana sites. It offers outstanding nearly 360-degree sweeping panoramic views. On land, the hills and valleys of green jungle give way to rugged and dramatic black basalt lava coastline. Out to sea, the deep blue ocean and white cresting waves are dramatically blasted into spray and mist as they pound against the jagged cliffs. This place looks like a living postcard from heaven.*

Koki Beach – *Scenic beach park with much cultural significance. Sand and ocean conditions vary greatly depending on season.*

Watch Maui Sunsets

When you are on Maui, you will notice how much people truly appreciate watching Maui sunset, both locals and visitors alike. It is the best way to end the day and begin the evening.

Sunsets on Maui are incredible and the best part is you can enjoy it for free. You can enjoy it from the ocean, from the lanai of your home or condo, or from Haleakala, which leads us to the next thing to do on Maui which is visiting Haleakala.

Visit Haleakala Mountain

Watching the sunrise is also extra special on Maui. There are many places you can enjoy the sunrise on the north and eastern side of the island. However, there is a special place worth going to and experiencing either Maui sunrise or sunset, and that is on Haleakala.

Haleakala is the mountain that makes up all of the eastern half of Maui. Its elevation is 10,023 feet and the crater at the top of this volcano is one of Maui's most incredible sights. The crater is seven and a half miles long, two and a half miles wide, and 3,000 feet deep.

The official website to go to is https://www.nps.gov/hale/index.htm

Haleakala Sunrise

I am sure that somewhere along the planning of your trip to Maui you have heard about Haleakala Sunrise. It is an incredible experience. You will arrive there at dark, then slowly the sun will rise and it is amazingly beautiful with the sky and clouds turning into various colors and sun coming up over the ocean and clouds and volcano crater below you.

I must warn you though that your "wow" experience will depend on the weather and the clouds. I have been up at Haleakala when the view is spectacular and remarkable. I have also been up there when it is wet, cloudy and there is not much to see. The best thing to do is to check the weather before you head up there. You can call the National Weather Service. Hotline for Haleakala Summit at 808-944-5025 ext. 4 for an up-to-date weather forecast.

Make a Reservation for Sunrise Viewing

The National Park Services for Haleakala requires a reservation for visitors in personal and rental vehicles to enter the Summit District from 3:00 am to 7:00 am to view the sunrise. The one day $1.50 sunrise reservation can be made up to 60 days in advance. The park entrance fee is separate and is payable during the day of the visit.

Effective January 1, 2020, the entrance **fees** to the **park** is $30 per vehicle, $25 per motorcycle and $15 per pedestrian or bicyclist. The receipt allows unlimited re-entry into either district of the **park** (Summit or Kipahulu) for three days.

The cost of a Tri-Park Pass, the annual pass that allows visitors unlimited entry to the three fee-collecting national parks in Hawaii (Hawaii Volcanoes National Park, Haleakala National Park and Puuhonua o Honaunau National Historical Park) also increased from $50 to $55 on January 1, 2020.

If you opt to go with a Tour Company to experience Haleakala sunrise, then you don't have to worry about reservation. They take care of that. Usually, the tour bus (or van) will pick you up at around 2am and will take you to the summit to go to the crater. Popular Haleakala Sunrise tours are by Valley Isle Excursion and Skyline Hawaii.

Haleakala Sunset

If you are not a morning person and waking up in the wee hours of the morning is just not for you, I highly recommend going to see the Haleakala sunset instead. Sunset at Haleakala with its warm colored clouds is breathtaking. Some visitors actually prefer Haleakala Sunset over Haleakala Sunrise. The bonus is that you don't have to make a reservation to watch the sunset.

Tips on Visiting Haleakala

1. **Dress Warm.** It is cold up at Haleakala so bring warm clothes for this. When you go there, wear pants, shoes, sweaters or jackets. Bring layers of clothing. You might also want to bring gloves, scarves and blankets. The visitor center at 7,000 feet has an average of high temperature of 59° F and low of 41° F in February.

2. **Schedule your sunrise visits for the first full day of your trip** (especially if you are coming from the East Coast and Midwest). On your first day of vacation your body clock is not on Hawaii Time yet so it won't be so hard to wake up at 2am or 3am in the morning.

3. **Bring Drinking Water.** For sunrise bring your coffee, tea or whatever warm drink you would want to take in the morning. There are no stores to buy drinks up at Haleakala National Park.

4. **Bring food if you are planning on staying longer to hike** or have a picnic somewhere in Kula. There are some restaurants in Kula on your way down such as Kula Lodge, Grandma's and La Provence.

5. **Fill up your gas tank before you head to Haleakala.** The last gas station is 27 miles below the summit at Pukalani. Fill up the night before if you are going for sunrise because it may be impossible to find an open gas station.

6. **Take note of the elegant Silversword Plants.** This silvery green plant called "ahinahina" is a distant relative of the sunflower. Each plant can grow for 3 years up to 50 years, but blooms only once in a lifetime. They are only found in Hawaii – here on Haleakala and on some volcanoes on the Big Island. Picking or otherwise disturbing a silversword is illegal. When hiking, do not wander off the trail to go closer to a silversword (because you must stay on the trail). If you want to see them up close, hike to the short Silversword Loop that veers off the Halemauu Trail.

7. **Watch out for the Nene.** Nene are also known as the Hawaiian Goose, and they are the official state bird and an endangered species whose only natural habitat is in the Hawaiian Islands. They are adorable and sometimes friendly, but if you encounter them during your stay on Maui, we ask that you admire them from afar and not feed them any "human food" for a variety of reasons. These birds are rare endangered species and under protection.

Headquarters Visitor Center

The Headquarters Visitor Center is 1 mile (1.6 km) past the Summit District entrance gate. Inside, park staff can answer questions at the information desk and issue backcountry permits when available. A small exhibit hall features displays on the park's natural and cultural history. The visitor center also houses a Hawaii Pacific Parks Association bookstore inside. Restrooms are accessible from the outside and are generally open 24/7. Please check park alerts for information on closures.

Haleakala Visitor Center

About a 30 minute drive from the Headquarters Visitor Center, the Haleakala Visitor Center is perched on the edge of the impressive volcanic valley. Inside, park staff can answer questions at the information desk. Visitors can learn about the history of the mountain through various displays. There is also a Hawaii Pacific Parks Association bookstore with souvenirs available for purchase. Restrooms are located nearby in a separate building and are open 24/7. Please check the alerts page for any closures.

Hiking and Coastal Walks

Hiking is a great way to explore Maui and enjoy its nature, especially during the pandemic because it is open air and naturally socially distanced. Other people, however, prefer a more casual coastal walk and that can be fun too. Below are some of the hikes and coastal walks you can enjoy on Maui.

Hiking:

1. **Sliding Sands at Haleakala National Park** is a moderate to difficult hike, depending upon how far travelers decide

to hike. The trail is not a loop, and it is eleven miles to do the full trail out and back; however, even after a half-mile, hikers can get gorgeous views of the crater, cinder cones, silverswords, and more. This hike is at 10,000 feet of elevation. On a clear day, hikers can get panoramic views of Maui, the crater floor, and neighbor islands. It is important to note that Sliding Sands lives up to its name. The hike is relatively easy on the descent into the Crater; however, if hikers decide to turn around and exit the way they entered, the hike becomes a bit more arduous as the sand trail can take a bit longer to hike uphill. A good footwear is important. Also, make sure to pack lots of water and sunscreen, as there is absolutely no shade on this spectacular hike.

2. **The Pipiwai Trail** is an easy-to-moderate hike that starts in the Kipahulu District of Haleakala National Park. The hike is roughly five miles out-and-back and takes hikers through an enchanting bamboo forest for a large portion of the journey. Along the way, visitors will pass numerous waterfalls, guava and lilikoi growing wild, an impressive photo-op at a banyan tree, and eventually reach the thick bamboo forest. Once at the bamboo, most of the journey follows boardwalk-style planks and ends at Waimoku Falls, an amazingly tall set of waterfalls. This trail may be on the long side for some, but the terrain is relatively easy and provides an amazingly wide variety of scenery throughout the hike.

3. **The Pali Trail,** also known to many as the "Hike to the Windmills," is a relatively challenging hike in Olowalu, on the way to West Maui. This trail takes travelers along a

five-mile journey through the West Maui Mountains to get up close and personal with giant windmills. The trail is a five-mile path with two trailheads and a few ways to do this hike. Many people will bring two vehicles, and park one at each trailhead and hike five miles one way. A more common option is to start at the trailhead found after the tunnel across from the Lahaina side and to hike 2.5 miles up to the windmills and return on the same route. Especially motivated hikers will sometimes turn this into a 10-mile hike, journeying the five miles one way and then tracing their steps back to the trailhead they started from. Regardless of the route chosen, hikers will want to pack ample water and sunscreen, as this can be a challenging hike with little-to-no shade along the way. While challenging, the hike offers beautiful panoramic views of Maui, the coast, Molokai, Lanai, and Molokini.

4. **Waihee Ridge** is a challenging hike with amazing views of valleys in the West Maui Mountains. The trailhead is easy to find and is located across from Mendes Ranch. When driving in, hikers will first pass through the overflow parking, and then follow a narrow-paved road up to the trailhead parking lot. This lot can often fill up by mid-morning, in which case visitors will need to return to the overflow parking. Be mindful that this will add additional activity time, as hikers will need to walk the paved road to the trailhead. Along the way, travelers may encounter cows and a variety of birds. Additionally, there are numerous overlook points that provide great views of the valleys and the coast. The hike is roughly five miles out-and-back and eventually brings visitors to a narrow ridge with man-made steps to reach the summit

point. This hike may not be for the faint-of-heart but it does provide beautiful and unique vantage points of Maui.

5. **Waihee Coastal Dunes and Wetlands Refuge** offers a two-mile coastal trail in a beautifully secluded wildlife refuge. This section of coast is a particular favorite of Hawaiian monk seals, and visitors often report sightings of the sea mammals resting on the shore. Visitors can expect a gentle stroll with gorgeous scenery on a protected (and therefore less-developed) shoreline.

6. **Polipoli** is a recreation area that takes hikers to new heights—literally! Located at an elevation of 6,200 feet, Polipoli has a variety of trails that can suit nearly any hiker. The drive can be arduous and a vehicle with high clearance and four-wheel drive is required to get to the trailhead. Due to the high elevation, it can actually get pretty chilly at Polipoli, so it would be a good idea to bring a sweatshirt or jacket.

7. **Hosmers Grove** is an easy half-mile loop located at the Hosmer's Grove Campground just inside of Haleakala National Park. This loop is relatively flat and takes hikers through a beautiful forest with a wide variety of trees and plants. The hike is one of the easier trails inside of Haleakala National Park and can be a great hike for families who are visiting the Crater.

8. **Makawao Forest Reserve** is a protected forest in Upcountry Maui and a great spot for a hike or a walk to take a break from the sun. Located in a thick, jungle-like forest, this series of

trails can keep hikers busy for a long time. Upon entering the park, visitors will travel a short journey along a trail to reach a trailhead with a map of the trails available. One of the most popular hikes is the five-mile loop trail that winds through the forest and slowly gains elevation. Along this path, hikers will find picnic tables at a few resting spots, so this can be a good spot to bring a small, packed lunch. Hikers should be mindful that Makawao Forest Reserve also welcomes mountain bikers and the biking and hiking trails often intersect. Mountain bikers and BMX riders will love this location, as it offers ample amounts of trails and a large BMX park with a series of jumps. While hiking Makawao Forest Reserve is not particularly difficult, it can take time as the trails are long and winding.

9. **Waihou Spring Forest Reserve (also known as the Olinda Forest)** is a hidden gem in Upcountry Maui. The trail consists of a short half-mile loop that travels through a pine forest. For a longer and more challenging journey, hikers can add on the Waihou Spring Trail, which is an additional mile out and back. This section takes hikers down steep switchbacks to the base of a natural spring, with small caves that can be explored. This section of the hike is popular among locals for exercise, as the journey back up from the spring can be tiring! Overall, the area is very well-maintained, and the main loop trail is a great spot for families.

10. **Iao Valley** is a beautiful, lush valley near Wailuku. The official hikes inside of Iao Valley are rather short and go along paved paths the entire way. Along these paths, visitors can see amazing and up-close views of the West Maui Mountains towering

above them, including one of Maui's most iconic landmarks: the Iao Needle. The trail will take hikers down to the Iao Stream, which is a great spot for a refreshing (but chilly!) dip in the river. Technically, the park only encompasses the short paved loop, but more adventurous hikers can follow a well-traveled and fairly defined path that goes along the Iao Stream.

11. **The Hoapili Trail at La Perouse Bay** Located in Makena, at the end of the road in South Maui, this trail offers a unique hiking experience, as travelers can journey through a massive lava-flow field created by age-old eruptions and hike along the ancient King's Trail. The journey is an out-and-back trail that will take hikers to secluded tide pools and beaches, eventually arriving at Kanaio Beach, which is a gorgeous salt-and-pepper colored beach. For most hikers, this is the turnaround point, although the King's Trail does continue much further around the backside of the island. Be warned that the trail can be much more difficult to follow once hikers have passed Kanaio Beach. Another option is to hike a short distance to one of the small, secluded beaches or tide pools for a relaxing, mostly private beach oasis. No matter the distance, hiking at La Perouse is a lot of fun, but hikers should know it is very sun-exposed and the terrain is rugged, so sturdy shoes and ample water are a must.

Coastal Walks

1. **The Wailea Coastal Walk** is a two-mile coastal walk in front of the Wailea resorts. The path can be picked up just outside of many of the hotels and resorts; however, parking

at Polo Beach, Wailea Beach, or Ulua Beach is typically the easiest way to access the path. Walkers and beachgoers will enjoy a long, paved walkway with very little incline, and it is complemented by spectacular views of Maui's most pristine beaches. Some especially lucky walkers may even spot some honu or dolphins playing in the surf! It can be a good idea to pack a small beach bag with a towel, as a dip in the ocean is the perfect reward after this two-mile walk or run!

2. **Kaanapali and Lahaina Coastal Walk** is a 1.4-mile path and one of the most popular walkways on Maui for good reason! This gentle walk begins at the Kaanapali Sheraton and travels along some of West Maui's most famed beaches. Its convenient resort location means that this path can get rather busy by midday and at sunset, so those looking for a more open walkway may want to be mindful of the time. Once walkers reach the end of the path, they have the option to continue their journey all the way through Wahikuli State Park and down to Front Street and Lahaina village for food and shopping. This can be a much longer journey, but a nice way to see Front Street without needing to find parking.

3. **Kapalua Coastal Walk** is a roughly 2-mile walk along the Kapalua Coast. The trail is gentle and well-traveled, providing visitors with great shoreline views and interesting rock formations to view along the way. Walkers will want to bring or apply sunscreen, as there is not much shade along this path.

4. **Honolua Bay** features a stunning footpath through an old-growth forest of giant trees, complete with beautiful mosses

and jungle vines dangling from the trees. Along the path, hikers may find Hawaiian ti plants, dragonfruit vines, lilikoi, and more. The walk is less than a mile and leads to the beautiful shore of Honolua Bay, which is one of the most beautiful snorkeling spots on Maui.

5. **Kealia Pond Coastal Boardwalk** is located along Kihei's beautiful Sugar Beach with stunning views of the West Maui Mountains. This coastal boardwalk doubles as a wildlife refuge for some of Hawaii's endangered bird species and is the largest natural pond on the island. The path is a flat wooden boardwalk that winds through a nationally protected wetland sanctuary where birds from Asia and North America come to winter, alongside a variety of endangered species. This is a great stop for birdwatchers looking for a unique setting. Along the way, walkers can stop to read a number of informative signs that will explain the environmental importance and uniqueness of Kealia Pond.

Whale Watching

It is Whale Season on Maui at the time I am writing this book, and what an exciting time it is!

Whale season on Maui is from December through April; the peak is around February and March. Humpback whales migrate to Maui to pass on their knowledge to the young and engage in nursing activities, calving and mating. Mothers nurse calves for almost a year. Calves do not stop growing until they are ten years old.

Learn more about Humpback whales here at Pacific Whale Foundation https://www.pacificwhale.org/pacific-whale-foundation/

Whales are mysterious and it is not known why they breach or what their songs and sounds communicate. The name of the Humpback describes the motion it makes when it prepares to dive and arches its back.

It's fun to watch the Humpback Whales on Maui. During Whale season you can actually spot them from the shore.

Almost all boats that operate from Maui combine whale-watching with their regular adventures from December through April.

Popular Boat cruises are Trilogy Excursion, Pacific Whale Foundation and the Pride of Maui. Some prefer a small boat or rafts to go whale watching so they can get closer. Some of the smaller boats or rafts are Redline Rafting, Blue Water Rafting and Ultimate Whale Watch and Snorkel.

However, it is important to note that boats, as well as Stand Up Paddlers, Kayaks and E-Foils are forbidden by Federal Law from getting closer than 100 yards. There is a huge fine for violating this law.

As I mentioned earlier, you don't have to go on a boat to see the Humpback Whales. You can watch them from the shores too. Humpback Whales love to frolic in the channel separating the Valley Isle from Molokai and Lanai. A great place to watch from land is at McGregor Point, the scenic lookout at in between Mile Marker 8 and 9 on the Honoapiilani Highway on the road to Lahaina.

The Road To Hana

Hana is a beautiful destination. It's not just the destination, it is the journey.

The Road to Hana is one of the most famous drives in the world. The winding, scenic drive leads to one of Maui's most remote communities and provides stunning, tropical imagery along the way. Getting to Hana is no quick journey; the trek is a winding road flanked by beautiful oceans and waterfalls, complete with hairpin turns, single-lane bridges, and intimidatingly close cliffs. All this considered, the drive can be done in as little as two hours from Kahului... but where's the fun in that?

Sometimes, visitors will take pride in how quickly they made it to Hana and back, and this always sounds more like a missed opportunity! Traveling to Hana isn't just about seeing the rural town; it's about many of the beautiful and unique stops along the way. There is so much to see, from gushing waterfalls and jungly hikes to fresh fruit stands and local food stands and trucks. If you are traveling to Hana, consider taking your time on the famed road. Plan out a few "must-see" stops and be prepared to make even more pitstops for an unforgettable trip on the Road to Hana.

Some people think the Road to Hana is an overrated tourist destination, while others think the drive is the best thing to do on Maui. Personally, I am in the latter camp, and I imagine that those who feel it is overrated haven't taken the time to experience all the journey has to offer. If it is your first time, there are a few things that may help make your Hana trip a good one. Make sure that you have the essentials before you leave. This means snacks, water, bathing suits, towels, sandals, hiking shoes, and most importantly: a full tank of gas (there is none along the way, and gas in Hana town is very expensive).

If you are looking for an easier drive, try starting very early in the morning. By mid-morning, the road can get rather crowded, which can make your travel time a little longer. Getting an early start is also a great idea if you plan to make a lot of stops along the way.

Be mindful of locals/traveling during a pandemic

Traveling to Hana is an unforgettable experience, but during the COVID-19 pandemic, it is important to be mindful and respectful to the vulnerable local community. Hana is a small, close-knit community, and it can be challenging to acquire resources in town. The residents of Hana have a small clinic, but it is not equipped to handle a mass influx of patients. Please be mindful of this if you decide to visit Hana during the COVID-19 pandemic, and practice kindness and respectful behavior by properly wearing your mask should you visit any of the town's local shops or restaurants; and also by not parking illegally. We are all trying our best to make it through the pandemic, and a little kindness, cooperation, and aloha can go a long way.

To drive or to take the tour? This is one of the most frequently asked questions.

One of the most frequently asked questions about the Road to Hana is whether to drive or take a tour bus. There isn't necessarily one clear answer to this, and the best choice will depend on a few variables.

Driving yourself has its perks if you like to make frequent stops and find things that are off-the-beaten-path. It also doesn't limit your time in Hana or at any of your pitstops. If you are confident driving windy, sometimes-crowded roads and like to travel at your own pace, then driving yourself is probably the way to go. The downside of taking your own car is that it can sometimes be stressful to make the drive and it can be a lot of wear-and-tear on the vehicle. The roads are narrow, there are many curves and sharp turns, and it is hard to find parking when you want to stop at waterfalls (you can get fined with $200.

If you do decide to drive yourself to Hana, be aware that there are often local travelers who drive the road often or even as their commute to work. Since they travel the road often, they are more comfortable with the terrain than a visitor would be. To avoid being the cause of unwanted traffic, pull off the road, and allow local drivers to pass you.

Taking a tour bus can be a more relaxing way to visit Hana, as they take away the stress of driving, finding parking, or knowing where to stop. That said, visitors should be aware that they might not be able to see everything they've read about in books or online. If you are a first-time visitor to Hana and you aren't necessarily confident in your ability to drive the long, winding road, taking a tour bus may be the ideal option for you.

Tour guides will stop at many of the most famous locations along the Road to Hana and will be able to answer questions along the way.

Neither driving yourself or taking a tour bus is necessarily the "better" option; it is simply important to consider how you prefer to travel and make an informed decision from there.

JULY 2021 UPDATE:

There is an ongoing effort to mitigate and relieve *traffic congestion's and illegal parking along the scenic route of The Road to Hana* that has grown with the recent return of tourism.

Signs along the Hāna Highway were installed to discourage illegal parking by warning of a $35 no parking fine and a $200 surcharge for illegal stopping on a state highway.

Sign installation began June 10 at the Waikamoi Stream Bridge at Mile 10. A total of approximately 70 signs are being placed along problem areas identified for the increased fines including: Waikamoi Stream Bridge; Twin Falls; Bamboo Forest; Ching's Pond; Waikani Bridge; Pua'a Ka'a Park; and Hanawī Bridge.

The Maui Police Department issued 387 parking citations and 83 warnings to violators on Hāna Highway between Ha'ikū and Hāna town over a three week period from June 1 and June 23. (MauiNewsNow.com)

Using GyPSy Guide App or Shaka Guide App recommended by many.

Some visitors who travel the Road to Hana swear by travel tools like GyPSy and Shaka Guide. These are apps that utilized GPS to take users on self-guided audio tours. The apps work all over the Hawaiian Islands, but many people use it along the Road to Hana for it is location-based narration. Another option is download the Road2Hana audio guide available at ther2h.com

The apps are available for purchase in Apple App and Google Play Stores, and come highly recommended for pit-stops due to their fun, informative, and entertaining narration. These apps can be a great in-between choice for visitors who want the information offered by tour guides but desire the freedom to travel at their own pace.

Bring a charging cord for your phone because these apps tend to drain your cell phone battery.

> July 2021 Update: As mentioned earlier in this section, there are fines and surcharges for illegal parking. I thought I should mention it again since I am not sure if the GyPSy and Shaka Guide Apps are updated on this no parking regulations.

The Road To Hana Stops Along The Way

I have mentioned making stops along the way many times in this chapter, but I realize that many visitors may not know where is worth stopping off. There are countless stops along the way, but in this section, I want to outline some of the most popular pitstops on the Road to Hana

Twin Falls: Twin Falls is a beautiful, easily-accessible waterfall just past the town of Haiku near Mile Marker 2. This is a great early morning stop and one that you will pass by early in your trip. There is a large sign marking the destination, and a large shoulder to park along the road. The walking path to Twin Falls is short, mostly flat, and well-maintained. Additionally, there are usually food trucks and there are port-a-potties (which may be the last restroom you find for a while).

Rainbow Eucalyptus Trees: Although this tree is not native to Hawaii, these gorgeous looking trees are often associated with the road to Hana. This little grove of rainbow eucalyptus tree around Mile Marker 6.7 is one of the most photographed stops on the road to Hana. What make this tree gorgeous? The tree barks are colorful: pastel red, pink, orange, green, gray and brown, various strokes running the length of each narrow tree. I heard one kid called it the "Crayola tree" and I agree. If you find it hard to find parking to atop at this grove, I recommend stopping by the Garden of Eden Arboretum. It is a more convenient way to be up close with the Rainbow Eucalyptus trees.

Garden of Eden Arboretum: The Garden of Eden Arboretum is the perfect place to stop and smell the flowers...literally! This spot is a gorgeous, beautifully maintained garden oasis near Mile Marker 10 and it will have any plant fan swooning. Visitors can walk the property at their leisure, enjoy a tropical smoothie in the Garden Cafe, or just enjoy the calming environment. Some of the more adventurous travelers may choose to rappel down the Puohokama Waterfall here by booking time with a guide for a fun and safe adventure. The cost to enter the arboretum is $15, and it is well worth it!

Keanae Peninsula: Keanae Peninsula is a gorgeous, rocky peninsula along the Road to Hana. You'll find the turn to the Peninsula on the ocean side between mile markers 16 and 17. Here, you'll discover historic buildings and a lovely chapel by a large, open field. This can be a great spot to stretch your legs and have a snack while enjoying some old Hawaiiana architecture and charm.

In Keanae, you'll find Aunty Sandy's Banana Bread stand. There's more to try than just banana bread, though. Aunty Sandy's offers fresh fruit, other baked goods, hot dogs, and more. This is one of the most popular spots along the Road to Hana and the banana bread sells quickly, so if you want to try Aunty Sandy's, you're going to want to get there early!

It is important to note that while it is a popular tourist pull-off, Keanae is also home to a small community, so please visit respectfully.

Upper Waikani Falls (Three Bears Waterfalls): Upper Waikani Falls is also known as Three Bears, as it is a series of three uniquely-sized waterfalls near Mile Marker 19. This is a very famous photo-op along the Road to Hana, and a sight that you won't soon forget. If you'd like to stop here, I would recommend starting your journey early in the day, as there is very little parking and it is almost always occupied by mid-morning. Whether you plan to stop and explore or not, be prepared to at least slow down and get a good look!

Coconut Glen's Ice Cream – If you're looking for a quick, refreshing treat as you journey the Road to Hana, you might want to check out Coconut Glen's ice cream around Mile Marker 27.5. The dairy-free ice cream is made fresh on-site and there are typically several tasty, locally-inspired flavors. Try their coconut candy topping!

Nahiku Marketplace – A good place to stop for a meal and do a little souvenir shopping is the Nahiku Marketplace along Mile Marker 28.7. This is a warm and welcoming local strip mall in the forest with a surprising selection of food. There you will also find Nahiku Café which has good coffee and excellent Lilikoi bars.

Waianapanapa State Park – Popularly known for its "black sand beach". At the beach overlook is one of the most iconic vistas on the drive to Hana with its sparkling blue ocean, shiny black sand, and lush green jungle background.

Important to note: Effective March 1, 2021, reservations are required to stop at Waianapanapa State Park. *Why?* Traffic and crowds have been getting a little out of control in recent years, so in an effort to preserve the local pace of life (and to make it more pleasant for the visitors), the reservation system will attempt to put a cap on the number of daily visitors.

Reservations can currently be made up to 14 days in advance online at **GoWaianapanapa.com**. No daily walk ins available. There are currently four time slots to choose from: 7am to 10am, 10am to 12:30pm, 12:30pm to 3pm and 3pm to 6pm. Admission is now set at $10/car for parking or $5 for walking in (no car) – which is paid when you make your reservation.

Beyond Hana Town

Many visitors will drive to Hana Town and then turn around, but did you know there is plenty more island to explore beyond Hana?

Just past the town, visitors can find Hamoa Beach, which is consistently ranked as one of the world's most beautiful beaches. It is a crescent-shaped white sand beach, perfect for relaxing or swimming in the surf. Despite its reputation, this beautiful beach isn't typically too crowded; however, be aware that parking is limited nearby.

Visitors can continue driving thirty minutes past Hana Town to reach Kipahulu, where they will find the second entrance to Haleakala National Park. At the Kipahulu District of Haleakala, sightseers can visit the Pools at 'Ohe'o, also known as Seven Sacred Pools. There is a short and gentle hike down to the famed pools. Those looking for a longer adventure can hike the popular Pipiwai Trail, which takes visitors along a meandering trail through guava trees, over rivers, and through tall bamboo, ultimately leading to Waimoku Falls. The hike is an unforgettable five-mile journey, and while the terrain is relatively easy, you may want to bring water, snacks, and good shoes!

Beyond Kipahulu, there are not very many stops; however, some adventurous drivers will choose to drive "the backside" which leads to Upcountry Maui and turns the Road to Hana into a loop. This road is bumpy and unpaved in sections, and rental car companies typically do not allow their cars to be taken on this road; although some local companies may allow it at the driver's own risk. The drive along the backside is typically very dry and provides spectacular ocean views, plus occasional rural pitstops like the Kaupo General Store. You'll pass through farm land that is grazed by cattle herds that sometimes make their way into the road, so be alert while driving. If you choose this more adventurous and sometimes challenging route, be prepared to drive slowly and carefully.

Farm Tours and Eco Tours

1. **Alii Kula Lavender Farm** is a great place to visit upcountry. They grow expansive lavender fields alongside many other rare and beautiful tropical plants. In addition to the scenery, make sure to try some of their lavender products, including scones, coffee, tea, and macarons. Currently, Alii Kula Lavender Farm closed due to COVID-19 restrictions but re-opened recently with limited days and hours, Friday to Sunday.

2. **Surfing Goat Dairy Farm** is a certified humane goat farm located in Kula. The farm offers visitors a behind-the-scenes look at goat herding and dairy farming. At Surfing Goat, visitors can experience a variety of tours. The Casual Tour is perfect for visitors on a time crunch and allows access to the farm and a brief tour, during which attendees can meet some goats. Another option is the Evening Chores Tour, a fun and hands-on experience that allows guests to assist in milking goats and putting them to bed in the evening. For those looking for an even more in-depth tour, there is the Grand Dairy Tour. This interactive option lets visitors learn how to care for goats, how to craft delicious goat cheeses, and even get some hands-on experience with milking goats. Reservations are required for tours and Surfing Goat Dairy is open Tuesday through Saturday from 10:00am to 4:00pm.

3. **Ocean Vodka** is a locally distilled vodka, and the company offers an in-depth tasting and farm tour. Ocean Vodka is created using sugarcane, and the tour takes visitors through

sugar cane fields and then into the distillery in order to understand the full process from start to finish.

4. **Ulupalakua Tour.** Maui Wine is located upcountry in Ulupalukua. While this can be a long drive, it is certainly worth it. Visitors can walk through the vineyards on a very informative farm tour, and then enjoy a glass of locally sourced and produced wine in the Tasting Room. The grounds are large and beautifully maintained, so a visit to Maui Wine can be a wonderfully relaxing afternoon while on Maui.

5. **Kula Country Farms** grows and sells a wide variety of produce, but they are best known for their you-pick strawberries and pumpkin patch in the fall. The farm is a great spot to stop for a snack while enjoying a day in Upcountry Maui, and the pumpkin patch is a can't-miss event every year. Kula Country Farms is open seven days a week, from 9:00am to 4:00pm.

6. **O'o Farm** offers two unique tours. One is a farm-to-table lunch tour where guests experience a meal source entirely with locally grown food. The other option is a "seed-to-cup" coffee tour, in which participants can learn the history and agriculture around coffee while enjoying some freshly harvested and brewed coffee. Both tours are by reservation.

7. **Maui Alpaca Farm** offers a variety of personalized, private tours and activities at their farm in Makawao. Visitors can get up close and personal with the beautiful alpacas during picnics, yoga classes, healing sessions and more.

8. **Maui Butterfly Farm** is located in Olowalu and offers a unique experience to visitors who may want to see beautiful butterflies up close while learning more about these gentle insects. The farm offers tours by appointment and is open every day from 10:00am to 1:00pm.

9. **Leilani Farm Sanctuary** is a large animal sanctuary located in Haiku. The Sanctuary is home to all types of rescued animals, including goats, cats, geese, donkeys, sheep, rabbits, tortoises, pigs, ducks, deer, and even a cow. While visiting, guests can meet the animals or simply enjoy the beautiful and peaceful setting. The farm is a lush, tropical oasis and offers tours by appointment on Saturdays at 10:00am.

10. **Maui Chocolate** offers an in-depth tour of their cacao farm, as well as a chocolate tasting in their facility. Maui Chocolate is a locally grown and produced chocolate on Maui, and their facility is a great stop for the whole family. Tours are by appointment.

Luau

Old Lahaina Luau is the most popular Luau on Maui and I highly recommend it. It is truly entertaining and has the Hawaiian feel. They just recently re-opened. They are strictly implementing safety protocols. When you visit their website at www.oldlahainaluau.com you will see a page on their Enhanced Health and Safety Measures. It was well thought of and written which will give you confidence that going to their event will be safe. If you have previously attended the Old Lahaina Luau, you will recognize the difference in their 2021 program. Food and drinks are served (no more buffets), there are revised seating arrangements to abide by the social distancing measures, and masks are required unless you are eating or drinking.

There are other luaus open and I highly recommend that you call them first before making reservations online just to double check. Prices and procedures change often during pandemic.

Here is a quick list of current luaus on Maui in addition to the Old Lahaina Luau:

- Andaz Luau (The Feast at Mokapu)
- Marriott Luau (Te Au Moana)
- Royal Lahaina Luau (Myths of Maui Luau)
- Grand Wailea Luau (Ahaaina Wailea Luau)
- Feast At Lele (at 505 Front Street, Lahaina)
- Hyatt Luau (Drums of the Pacific)
- Maui's Finest Luau – New Luau, currently hosted at the beautiful Olowalu Plantation House.
- Sheraton Luau (Maui Nui Luau)

Website to check and go to for Maui Luau Information: www. mauiluau.com

Interest Related Activities

There are many more things to do on Maui that I won't discuss the details. If any of these are of interest to you, check out https://activityauthority.com or https://www.mauiinformationguide.com for additional information:

- Golfing
- Fishing
- Tennis
- Zip Lining
- Visit Maui Ocean Center
- Visit Historical and Cultural Sites
- Mystery Maui Escape Room
- Fly a Private Plane
- Helicopter Ride
- Go to the Spa

Sunset at Haleakala - December 25, 2020

PERSONAL NOTES AND PLANNING

CHAPTER 6

MEMORABLE MAUI DINING AND LOCAL GRINDZ

Warning: This chapter is going to make you hungry! There are so many delicious foods on Maui. There are also numerous restaurants to choose from, which made this chapter difficult to write.

I got stuck in this chapter during the writing process. I originally had a very long list of places to eat. I wanted to include all the restaurants in each town, and give you specific recommendations on what to order. In the end, I had to remind myself that it is an impossible task for me. I needed to simplify, so I did.

In line with the goal of this book, I am highlighting the restaurants that are currently highly recommended by me and the members of Visit Live Love Maui Facebook group. I shared a bit more about places to eat in Kihei because I live here and are very familiar with them.

Where to Eat on the South Side

Wailea/Makena

For Fine Dining, **Ferraro's** at Four Seasons Maui, **Morimoto's** at Andaz, **Nick's Fishmarket** at Fairmont Kealani, **Humble Market Kitchin by Roy Yamaguchi** at Wailea Beach Marriott and **Ko Restaurant**, also at Fairmont Kealani are highly recommended.

For a more casual dining (but not too casual), **Wailea Kitchen** is the new place to go. It is under new management. It is located next to the Wailea Tennis Courts. It is like a big open air covered lanai. Good food and drinks, with a tag line "clean food, dirty drinks". Other choices for dinner are **Lineage, Longhi's** and **Tommy Bahamas**, all located at The Shops at Wailea.

One new favorite place for breakfast or brunch is actually a coffee shop at Wailea Village: the **Akamai Coffee Shop**. It has the perfect location and set up in addition to great coffee. They have outdoor tables located on the lanai which are ideal for social distancing. When in Wailea, this is definitely a good stop. It is a convenient and nice place to meet a friend, or even a client.

Monkeypod re-opened and many are happy about it. Their Lilikoi Mai Tai is the most popular Mai Tai on Maui! **Pita Paradise** is also open at the Wailea Gateway. We highly recommend them too! Fresh Fish and good Mediterranean dishes. Parking used to be a problem at the Wailea Gateway, but not at this time.

Mulligan's on the Blue is open for lunch and happy hour/dinner. Mulligan's is open-air Irish-American restaurant & bar at Wailea Blue Course offering live music & ocean views.

Manoli's Pizza Co. is open for fresco dining. Manoli's is family-owned restaurant & bar serving pizza, drinks & Greek appetizers with open-air seating.

For casual "mostly *to-go* or *carry-out* dining", you can go to **Island Gourmet Market** at the Shops at Wailea. They do have a few tables inside and a few outside facing the parking lot. Another quick option is **The Market Maui** the Wailea Gateway Center.

Kihei

Five Palms Restaurant has the best oceanfront location in South Maui. Overlooking the stunning coastlines of Keawakapu Beach, Five Palms Restaurant features innovative Maui Coastal cuisine accompanied by spectacular sunsets over the sparkling blue waters of the Pacific Ocean. During winter, you might even see whales on the horizon! My family loves going here for breakfast but it is also great for lunch and dinner. Their outdoor covered lanai ("lanai" is the Hawaiian term we use for deck or patio) is a perfect set up for restaurants during Covid19 pandemic so they are among the few restaurants to have dine-in available during pandemic

Kihei Café is very popular among visitors and locals alike. Known for their delicious breakfast with big servings, especially the pancakes and Loco Mocco. Located across from Kalama Park with a set-up that looks like a Parisian outdoor café (open air tables under canopies).

Coconuts Fish Café is a family-friendly restaurant that serves excellent food. This is our family's go to restaurant. I especially love their fish tacos which is not like a regular taco – it has fresh mangoes on it! Fish tacos is their famous meal but also try Mahi mahi sandwich or Ono on a Bun – they are truly ono (delicious!). They have 2 locations in Kihei, one at Azeka Shopping Center, and one at Kamaole Shopping Center. During the pandemic, they have closed the inside dining and maximized the to go services. Recently, the Kamaole Shopping location are utilizing the wide-open air lanai in their building for "dine-in" as they arranged seating areas on the hallways.

Paia Fish Café is another place to order delicious fish tacos and fish sandwiches. They also have an open lanai for dine-in. Located at the Kalama Shopping Center across from Kalama Park in Kihei.

Café O'lei is another good recommendation with good food and local favorites. However, their restaurant in Rainbow Mall does not have an open-air setting so with social distancing guidelines, their capacity is limited. If you prefer an open air setting during pandemic (which is what is recommended) then go to their sister restaurant in Kihei, the Ami Ami, located at Maui Coast Hotel along South Kihei Road.

Maui Brewing Company is not just a place for beer. They have a restaurant in this brewery headquarter that serves delicious island-inspired cuisines. Our friends at The Aloha 360 Podcast highly recommends this place. They have an expansive outdoor garden seating and open-air interior which are perfect setting for dining during pandemic.

Fabiani's is located in Kihei and specializes in Baked Goods and Pizzas, but they have a variety of food and drinks as well. The other is an Italian Restaurant at the Wailea Gateway Center. During Covid19 pandemic, they converted their open lanai space for kids' playroom, into an outdoor dining set-up. They did a good job expanding their capacity so more people can enjoy their delicious food.

Havens is a new Noodle and Smash Burger place in Kihei that recently opened during pandemic. It is Take-out only. Already a local favorite even just within a couple weeks of opening, Havens is making waves in the Maui community. This is a "must try" for visitors. Located in Kihei behind the Shell gas station along Piilani Highway. I highly recommend calling in your order 20 minutes before you want to pick-up your food because they are always busy. It's a Noodle and Smash Burger haven. Definitely something great that came out of pandemic. My favorite is Fried Noodles and Chow Fun. So flavorful!

There are so many more great places to eat in Kihei. I decided to just add quick list in addition to what I previously mentioned. Here it is for your reference.

- **Cuatro** – Offering a mix of Asian Latin Fusion and local fish daily.
- **Isana** – Fresh caught fish, sushi and island cuisine
- **808Deli** – Voted Best Local Sandwich every year since 2008. Their freshly made pudding is great too!

- **Hawaiian Moons Natural Food Store** – Deli section is a great addition to this Natural Food grocery
- **Cinnamon Roll Place** – Best cinnamon rolls on the island made fresh every morning.
- **That's A Wrap** – Just a cool little café with vegan and gluten free options.
- **Kamana Kitchen** – good Indian Food with big lanai space for outside dining.
- **Ami –Ami** – relaxed eatery offering traditional meat and seafood dishes in modern space with patio.
- **Akamai Coffee** – more about this on coffee on Wailea Section
- **Fred's Mexican Café** – Mexican Food and Great ocean view of Kamaole Beach II
- **Amigo's** – our go to for Mexican food in Kihei. I like their Shrimp Ceviche
- **Piko Café** – more about this on coffee on Maui Section. Great place to order Loco Moco.
- **Shaka Pizza and Pizza Madness** – Both good places to get Pizza in Kihei

Azeka's Shopping Center:

- **Coconut's Fish Café** – Known for their fish taco with mango
- **Miso Phat** – Fresh Sushi and Sashimi
- **Roasted Chiles** – Mexican restaurant known for their mole
- **Fork and Salad** – Locally sourced ingredients. Great salad and they have delicious soup too.
- **Panda Express** – Fast food known for their Orange Chicken Beef Broccoli and Walnut Shrimp

- **Wow Wow Lemonade** – Craft Lemonades, Acai Bowl and Smoothies
- **Peggy Sue's Maui** – 1950's style atmosphere serving hamburgers, hotdogs, milkshakes, etc.
- **Java Café** – Coffee, Cold Press Juices and smoothies
- **Diamonds Bar** – Sports Bar and Grill

Azeka's Shopping Center:

- **Homemade Bakery Maui** – yummy warm malasadas in the morning
- **Maui Pie** – Lilikoi Pie is delicious!
- **Nutcharee's Thai Food** – Started being famous in Hana and now they have Kihei location. I always order Green Mango salad when I go there.
- **Nalu's** – Locals favorite, try their ahi sandwich, ahi eggs benedict and ahi poke bowl.

Kihei Kalama Shopping Center:

- **Kihei Café** – Famous breakfast place in Kihei across the street from Kalama Park. They offer delicious pancakes, homestyle omelettes, and one of the best places to get Loco Moco.
- **Threes Bar and Grill** – Wailea dining at Kihei prices is their tag line. Innovative and creative dishes – delicious food at a good price.
- **Paia Fish Company** – Lots of open air seating. Good Fish Tacos and Fish Sandwiches.

- **Tiki Lounge** – Place to go for casual Happy Hour. They serve NY style pizza handcrafted from scratch with fresh local ingredients.

Kukui Mall Shopping Center:

- **Thailand Cuisine** – our go to for Evil Prince Dish
- **Outrigger Pizza** – Food Truck at Kukui Mall Parking lot
- **Sansei** – Famous place for sushi. During COVID-19 they moved to a new and bigger place in Kukui Mall.

Piilani Food Court:

- **Bale** – Vietnamese Fast Food.
- **Aloha Thai Food** – Good Thai Food.
- **Maui Burger** – Locally sourced, freshly cooked
- **L & L – Local and Hawaiian Fast Food.** Good to get Plate Lunches with big portions.
- **Subway** – in case you just want a sub sandwich

Where to Eat on the West Side

Merriman's Ocean Point Grill is one of the most popular restaurants during the pandemic. Their beautiful open air set up next to the beach is absolutely fantastic. And if you are craving the Monkeypod Mai Tai you go to Merriman's Oceanpoint Grill and you can order that same Lilikoi Mai Tai there (yes, they have the same owner). Needless to say, the food is excellent!

The next popular restaurant is **Mala's Ocean Tavern** on Front Street Lahaina. This place has grown during the Pandemic. A great ocean-front place with delicious food, wonderful wine and creative culinary cocktails. They actually converted their parking lot into an open-air dining and it turned out fabulous!

Sea House in Napili next to Napili Bay. Known for its stunning ocean view and epic sunset during dinner so reserve early and get a good seat. In addition to the view, enjoy a delicious sea-to-table cuisine.

Another open-air restaurant next to the ocean is the **Pacifico on the Beach**. They are open Thursday to Monday 5pm to 7pm. Located at 505 Front Street in Lahaina.

Kimo's Maui Most of you already know they have great food and a gorgeous ocean view. And one thing they are also known for? The HULA PIE! It is home to the original Hula Pie. It's not to be missed!

Papa Aina in Pioneer Inn has been creative. Their new chef, Lee Anne Wong has been hosting creative and fun dinners with theme. This is a must experience especially for foodies and also for those who love history. The Pioneer Inn is Maui's oldest hotel and eatery, established in 1901. Papa Aina is open 8am to 2 pm daily and Friday Dinner is at 6pm.

Hula Grill and Leilani's – Both are located at the Whaler's Village in Kaanapali. Both also have beautiful ocean views, delicious cuisine and Hula Pies! When our family and friends come to visit Maui, we always take them to Hula Grill and/or Leilani's. Hula Pie is a must try dessert!

Star Noodle re-opened on a new location at 1285 Front St. in Lahaina. It is the former location of Aloha Mix Plate. Aloha Mix Plate is temporarily closed. Star Noodles is open seven days a week 10:30am to 10pm. Great ocean view while you eat delicious food.

Other good places to dine are:

- **Gazebo's** – Famous for its breakfast. There is usually a long line so come early.
- **Roy's at Kaanapali** – one of our favorites
- **Moku Roots** – Vegan food that even non-vegan loves. A must try!
- **Down the Hatch** – a fun place with good food and drinks. It is a seafood/restaurant bar serving breakfast, lunch, happy hour (2-5pm), dinner and late night.
- **The Fond** – serves Hawaiian Regional and New American Cuisine.
- **Joey's Kitchen** – Hawaiian Inspired Filipino Asian Cuisine, now on two locations: Napili Plaza and Whaler's Village in Kaanapali.
- **Pour House at Kapalua** – this is an upscale restaurant for Italian cuisine with local ingredients, plue craft cocktails and global wines.
- **Fleetwoods on Front Street** – American restaurant with a rooftop bar offering ocean views.

Where to Eat at Upcountry Maui

Kula Lodge – The Kula Lodge has been a favorite of both visitors and Maui residents for great dining experience and breathtaking views of Maui. Perched high above the green hills of Kula on the Valley Island of Maui, the Kula Lodge and Restaurant is a comfortable place to relax on the way back from Haleakala, Hana or Maui's Ulupalakua Winery. Arriving from the other direction, the Kula Lodge is a gateway to rich scenery of Upcountry Maui, a wonderful place to meet or treat your friends and the only full-service bar in Kula. During the pandemic, their outdoor seating is a big hit. There you can enjoy a perfectly social distanced delicious dining with marvelous view.

Kula Bistro – Located on the majestic slopes of Haleakala in beautiful Upcountry Maui, Kula Bistro offers fresh, flavorful cuisine in a casual family-style setting. Open daily for breakfast, lunch, and dinner, the bistro specializes in homestyle food with an Italian flair. Menu items range from classic entrées and local favorites to authentic pastas and pizzas. A decadent selection of homemade desserts and pastries are crafted daily.

Haliimaile General Store – You will find Haliimaile General Store a among the pineapple fields of Upcountry Maui. In this restaurant with a charming plantation vibe, you can enjoy the award-winning cuisine of Chef Beverly Gannon. Dishes are a unique blend of fresh Hawaiian flavor, local Asian influences, and modern preparations.

Freshies – Restaurant with fresh, locally-sourced ingredients. They have meaty, vegetarian, vegan and gluten-free food options. I actually have not been there yet, but my friends from The Aloha 360 Podcast love this place and highly recommend it. On my list to go to next time I go Upcountry Maui.

Other places to try are:

- **La Provence** (take out only)
- **Grandma's** (see section on Coffee and Breakfast for more info)
- **Sip Me** (see section on Coffee and Breakfast for more info)

Where to Eat in North Shore

Mama's Fish House – Arguably the most popular restaurant on Maui and the very best! In my opinion it is one of the best restaurants in the world. Located in a cove in Kuau, the oceanfront location is simply spectacular. The atmosphere is something you will remember including the beautiful tropical floral arrangements they have all around. Mama's Fish House serves outstanding fresh-catch and locally sourced cuisine. Prices are expensive but for me, it is definitely worth it. If you're on a budget, make sure to save for this dinner because you definitely wouldn't want to miss experiencing dining in at Mama's Fish House while on Maui.

Paia Fish Market – This restaurant has been a landmark in Paia since 1989. Known for their reasonable prices, excellent quality and large portions fresh fish and locally sourced ingredients. You can also find them in South Maui (Kihei) and West Maui (Lahaina) but this spot is Paia is the original. Order Fish Burgers and/or Seafood Pasta – oh they are so yummy!

Other places to eat:

- **Milagros**
- **Nuka**
- **Colleen's at the Cannery**

Where to Eat in Central Maui

- **Café O Lei** – There are two locations: one is at Maui Lani Golf Course and the other is at the former Mill House at the Maui Tropical Plantation.
- **Tin Roof** – a bustling local counter by Chef Sheldon Simeon serving pork belly bowls, garlic noodles, and other Hawaiian and Filipino and comfort fare. Curbside pick-up only at this time.
- **Alive and Well** – serving healthy food and sharing love for 22 years
- **Waikapu on 30** – Homemade deliciousness from best Pork Lau Lau to mouthwatering Sweet Potato Haupia Pie
- **Sam Satos** – One of Maui's best noodle house and definitely locals' favorite.
- **Saigon Café Maui** – a cozy, casual Vietnamese hideaway with delicious food, like shrimp soup cooked and served in a clay pot, and pho!
- **Poi by the Pound** – Poi is the star of their dishes but you can enjoy a vast variety of local dishes (See out section on Plate Lunches on Page 95). Since Da Kitchen in Kahului is closed, Poi By The Pound is the go to place in Kahului for local plate lunches and meals.

- **Koho**'s – Located at the Queen Kaahumanu Center

Coffee Shops, Breakfast and Brunch

One of my most popular blog post at A Maui Blog is about the Coffee Shops on Maui. Locals and Visitors alike loves coffee. While there are Starbucks and Coffee Bean and Tea Leaf here on Maui, I would like to share with you some of the local coffee spots you might want to try while visiting Maui. You can also order breakfast on Maui on some of these shops

Special thanks goes to Aloha Rise Coffee for their collaboration in writing this section. Visit their website at https://maui.coffee. We decided to organize the coffee shops according to towns/regions. You'll want to know what a good coffee place is close to where you're staying. So here they are: *please note they are not in any particular order or ranking.

South Maui

Piko Cafe – Piko Cafe is a small breakfast, lunch, and coffee joint tucked in the corner of the Azeka Center near Longs in Kihei. They serve some of the best local-style breakfasts and plate lunches, and they make a great cup of organic coffee to go along with it.

Cafe @ La Plage – Literally steps from "la plage," this charming cafe sits just across the street from the sand at Kamaole I. Guest at Cafe @ La Plage can expect to find great coffee from Maui Oma Coffee

Roasters, delicious breakfast sandwiches (almost all named after South Maui beaches), and a hearty dose of the aloha spirit.

Lava Java – Lava Java is a family-owned coffee shop that's been up and running since 2008. Located in Kihei Kalama Village, Lava Java makes a great stop to caffeinate before taking a surf lesson down the street at Cove Park. Lava Java also stocks an assortment of souvenirs and Maui grown coffee, including their famous Kula coffee.

Beach Street – Previously known as the *S&Q Kiosk*, Beach Street sits on South Kihei Road, on the corner in Rainbow Mall. Their menu features a variety of espresso drinks, breakfast items, shave ice, and tropical fruit smoothies.

Beachwalk – Not only does this sleek cafe on the Wailea Beach Path serve delicious espresso, but you'll also find snacks, sandwiches, and everything you might need for a beach day (sunscreen, rashguards, sunglasses – you name it). Overlooking Wailea Beach and boasting views of the West Maui Mountains and surrounding islands, this beachy cafe is home to potentially the best view to enjoy a morning coffee.

Akamai – With three locations serving 100% Maui coffee, Akamai has become one of the most popular places among both locals and visitors for a brew. Their first drive-through location has been a hit among locals since its inception, and Akamai's newer locations in South Maui have been successful as well.

Java Cafe – Formerly known as The Coffee Store, Java Cafe is located in the Kihei Azeka Shopping Center near Longs. This sleek cafe is known for its cold press juices, fresh pastries, and coffee. They also have an ample selection of 100% Maui and Kona coffee available for purchase.

That's A Wrap – This bright and airy cafe serves unique coffees and healthy colorful dishes infused with aloha. Add a shot of espresso to the red velvet latte, a combination of beetroot, vanilla, and cacao, or opt for the lavender cold brew. Located only steps from the beach at Kam II, That's A Wrap is a great place to refuel before or after a long beach day. It's also run by 2 of the coolest people on Maui. We love you Gina!

Kihei Caffe – Best known for their breakfasts, their blended "big Kahuna" for $7 is pretty famous. Bring cash and get ready for very big portions.

Kraken Coffee – Innovation, solid customer service, and dang good coffee are Kraken Coffee's M.O. Kraken is one of the few coffee trucks on Maui that boast drive-through service, the first on the island to start offering coffee ice cubes in cold drinks. Kraken Coffee has locations in Kihei (behind the Azeka shopping center) and Kahului (across from Costco).

The Market – Located downstairs from Monkeypod in the Wailea Gateway Center, The Market is a bona fide one-stop-shop. In addition to functioning as a coffee shop, The Market acts as a deli, eatery, and literal market. The Market stocks its shelves with locally roasted coffee beans from Origin Coffee Roasters, either for you to brew at home or as a gift for a coffee fan back home.

Honolulu Coffee Company – While Honolulu Coffee Company may not be locally owned, this growing coffee chain was born from humble beginnings – a coffee kiosk in downtown Honolulu – and their beans are grown just across the pond in Kona. You can find their delicious cuppas and various bagged coffees at their shops in the Hyatt Regency and Shops of Wailea.

Central Maui

Maui Coffee Roasters – Voted 'Maui's Best Coffee Shop' time and again by Maui Time Weekly readers, Maui Coffee Roasters in Kahului is the island's coffee hub. Maui Coffee Roasters roasts all of their beans on-site and serves their own freshly roasted coffee. Stop by for breakfast, lunch, or their "Happy Cappy" hour from 2 pm to close when cappuccinos are on special. Maui Coffee Roasters also sells an abundance of coffee and espresso gadgets, freshly roasted beans, and is a great place to shop for gifts for coffee lovers back home.

Maui Coffee Attic – This cozy mom and pop shop serves all-day breakfast, great coffee, and pastries with a local twist- try the ube scones or lilikoi croissants! Maui Coffee Attic is famous among Maui locals, as well as some of Maui's best local musicians. Maui Coffee Attic also hosts regular shows in their venue downstairs from the coffee shop.

Wailuku Coffee Company – Family owned and operated, Wailuku Coffee Company's flagship shop is nestled in the heart of the groovy Wailuku town on Market Street. In 2019, Wailuku Coffee Company expanded to Haiku, with a new shop in the Aloha Aina Center. Consistency is the name of the game at Wailuku Coffee

Company- their food and coffee are on point, and the flavor and presentation are the same from visit to visit.

Akamai Coffee Trailer – This is the original Akamai Coffee venue at the far end of the Home Depot parking lot in a small trailer.

West Side

The Coffee Store – Located in the quiet neighborhood of Napili, The Coffee Store is Maui's North-West shore's answer to coffee. Here you'll find some of the friendliest baristas on the island, fresh baked goods, and locally grown coffee. The Coffee Store is one of the last stops for coffee before heading towards Kahakuloa.

Belle Surf Cafe – Belle Surf Cafe is a tropical bohemian paradise, nestled in the heart of Lahaina Town. Here you'll not only find a plethora of organic eats like smoothie bowls and chia cups but some of the most deliciously unique coffee concoctions on Maui as well. The orange cardamom latte is a definite winner- espresso with orange zest, melted honey, cardamom, and textured milk over ice.

Island Vintage Coffee – Island Vintage Coffee has several locations around Hawaii; on Maui, they are located in Whaler's Village in Ka'anapali. This bustling cafe serves 100% Kona coffee, as well as acai bowls, bagels, and some local style breakfasts. Try the mouth-watering Mauna Kea iced coffee, complete with gelato, caramel, and black Hawaiian sea salt.

Island Press Coffee – Great local coffee and a taste of old Hawaii can be found at Island Press Coffee in Ka'anapali. Island Press Coffee serves coffee that was grown just up the road at the Ka'anapali coffee farm. They also have a collection of local kombucha on tap.

Hawaiian Village Coffee – Some of the island's best baristas work here. Not only is the coffee delicious, the latte art spectacular, but the customer service is outstanding as well. This could be why the cafe is often so busy, yet the service is undeniably quick. Hawaiian Village Coffee can also ship up to six pounds of locally grown coffee straight to your door.

Cafe Cafe – This quaint coffee shop in Lahaina has been voted Best Coffee Shop on Maui in years past by Maui Time Weekly readers. Tucked down Lahainaluna Road, a small side street off Front Street's main drag, Cafe Cafe is one of Lahaina's best-kept secrets and offers a lovely surprise for those who stumble upon it.

Maui Island Coffee – Established in 1992, Maui Island Coffee is the Lahaina go-to for fresh, locally roasted coffee. Maui Island Coffee purchases their beans from small coffee farms around Hawaii then roasts their beans in batches daily to ensure the best quality. You can find Maui Island Coffee in the Wharf Cinema Center across from the Banyan Tree in Lahaina.

Bad Ass Coffee – With two locations on Maui's west side (Lahaina on Front Street and Honokowai), Bad Ass serves as Maui's emporium for Hawaii-grown coffee. In addition to international brews, you'll find their shelves stocked with 100% Kona coffee, as well as coffee grown on Maui, Kauai, and the Ka'u region of the Big Island. Both locations also feature a variety of signature lattes, like the Menehune Mocha, with dark chocolate and raspberry.

North Shore and Upcountry

Grandma's – Grandma's Coffee House in Keokea is home to some of the world's best organic coffee. Grown on Maui, their coffee beans are handpicked, pulped, and naturally sun-dried before being hulled and roasted in house. Their 100+-year-old roaster is even visible through a display window next to the counter. Grandma's also serves fantastic food- their loco moco is one of the best on the island.

Paia Bay Café – This tropical oasis of a cafe serves a wide variety of coffee drinks, from creative lattes to a simple 100% Maui Mokka Peaberry. Pa'ia Bay Coffee is also home to one of the best breakfasts on the north shore. This coffee joint transforms into a lively bar in the evening, complete with a substantial dinner menu and live music.

Sip Me – Off Baldwin Avenue in Makawao Town, Sip Me is a cute and chic coffee shop serving coffee, juices, and sweet and savory treats. Their loose-leaf teas and their unique rose gold latte are a hit among regulars, and you'll often find tasty coffee specials. Sip Me stays true to their Maui roots by sourcing local organic ingredients for their juices and smoothies and serves coffee from local roasting company Maui Oma.

Espresso Mafia – Located across the street from Rodeo General Store in a small courtyard, Espresso Mafia is the newest coffee joint to hit Makawao Town. This coffee truck is locally owned and operated by a husband and wife team. With a handful of drink specials, homemade non-dairy "mafia milk," and expert knowledge of espresso, you'll be hard-pressed to find a better coffee on Maui. Try their honey cream latte with "mafia milk" or their lavender latte.

Better Things – Better Things is the latest cafe to open in Paia, located across the street from the post office on Baldwin Avenue in a whitewashed building. This spacious, aesthetically pleasing cafe is best known for its deconstructed iced latte, served with coffee ice cubes, and vegan takes on not-so-healthy items like pop tarts and donuts. Better Things serves coffee from a local roasting company, Social Hour Coffee Roasters.

Alba's Cuban Coladas – This tiny coffee truck in the Kulamalu Town Center in Pukalani packs a serious caffeine punch. Alba's serves authentic Cuban coffee (known for its potency) and traditional Cuban eats like empanadas.

Paia Bowls – This cute outdoor garden cafe serves açaí bowls, juices, smoothies, and great coffee from Maui Oma Coffee Roasters. Try their Beauty Rush "super coffee," blended with coconut milk, cacao creamer, and pearl powder, which helps to strengthen hair and nails and helps even skin tone. Only steps from Paia Bay, take your bowl and coffee-to-go and enjoy breakfast on the beach.

Local Food Favorites

Hawaiian Plate Lunch – Hawaiian plate lunch mainly features foods that were eaten by ancient Hawaiians (with some exceptions).

    a. *Chicken Long Rice* is made with rice noodles in chicken broth and usually has chunks of chicken, onion, and ginger in the broth, with cut green onions on the top. In plate lunch, chicken long rice is normally served with the noodles and chicken scooped from the broth, instead of as a soup. This is one of my favorite noodle soups.

b.   *Squid Luau* is squid cooked while wrapped in taro leaves (luau). Taro features heavily in traditional Hawaiian cooking. I enjoy eating squid luau and I often order it at Poi By The Pound restaurant in Kahului.

c.   *Poi* is pounded taro root. For first timers, it can be a bit bitter or a little sour but well-made poi is delicious; many people dip kalua pig or squid luau into poi, or mix in rice, as a flavor enhancer. However, poi can also be eaten by itself, as it is one of the most balanced foods on the planet.

d.   *Lau lau* is similar to squid luau. However, lau lau is normally steamed. The taro leaves are usually wrapped around pork (occasionally chicken) and salted butterfish.

e.   *Lomi-lomi* is a kind of tomato and salmon salad, with raw salted salmon mixed with tomato, onion, and other ingredients. Lomi-lomi salmon is one of the earliest dishes in Hawaiian cooking to feature Western ingredients, as tomatoes were introduced by early sailors visiting the islands.

Pre-pandemic, these Hawaiian Plate Lunches were served at popular restaurants including Aloha Mix Plate, Da Kitchen and Poi by The Pound. At the time of writing, only **Poi by the Pound** has re-opened.

I recommend going to **Waikapu on 30**. This is a local eatery across the road from Maui Tropical Plantation. They serve local food truly made by local folks. My favorite there are Luau Stew and Haupia Pie.

Local Plate Lunch includes foods from around the world, including Japan, the United States, Portugal, and many more nations. Some of the common dishes found in a plate lunch are:

a. *Teriyaki Beef* is one of the most popular entrees in plate lunch (followed by shoyu chicken, consisting of baked chicken marinated in a soy sauce-based marinade). Teriyaki beef is normally cooked in thin strips.

b. *Chicken Katsu* is a Japanese bread-crumb fried chicken dish served with katsu, a tomato-based sauce you can use for dipping or pouring over the chicken itself.

c. *Mac Salad* is a customary side dish for mixed-plate and is served cold.

d *Rice* is a part of almost every plate lunch and is often found in Hawaiian plate lunch as well (though not always, as rice was introduced from Asia and is not part of traditional Hawaiian cuisine).

e. *Chili* in Hawaii is normally served over rice.

Similar to the Hawaiian Lunch Plate, the Local Plate Lunches are available at Poi by the Pound and Waikapu on 30. There are also many Food Trucks serving Local Plate Lunches.

Poke *(pronounced Po-kay)* is cubed, salted raw ahi tuna Traditional poke only included salt, seaweed, and Maui onion, but you can now find poke with a variety of fish, seafood, sauces, and toppings.

For you who are not used to eating raw fish, this is a local dish to start with. With all the rich tasty flavors added, you won't even remember you are eating raw fish. Try it, you might actually really like it.

Oh ... Poke are available in many places, so the question is *where are the best places to get Poke?* In Kihei, I'd say Tamura's, South Maui Fish Co., Times Supermarket and Safeway, and also at Eskimo Candy. If you're staying in Wailea and didn't want to go to Kihei, they also sell Poke at Island Gourmet Market and Whalers General Store – both are at The Shops at Wailea.

On the West Side, a good place to get Poke is at Fish Market at Honokawai and Foodland. In Central, you can try Tin Roof in Kahului and Takamiya Market (where many locals go) homin Wailuku. Upcountry, go to Pukalani Superette.

Chow Fun is a local twist on a Chinese noodle dish and is served either in conjunction with mixed plate or even on its own. It is fun to get Chow Fun on Maui County fair and other Fundraising Events. Since there are no big events right now, you can find them on local restaurants and Food Trucks (there is a Food Truck place across from Costco Gas Station that serves Chow Fun and Plate Lunches)

Spam Musubi – Musubi is a Japanese snack food that consists of meat and sticky rice (not sushi rice) wrapped with nori (seaweed). In Hawaii, the most common variety is Spam musubi. The Spam is usually cooked in some kind of teriyaki sauce. You can find spam musubi at Foodland, ABC Stores and General Whalers Store. The best Spam Musubi I have tasted is from Sugar Beach Bakery in Kihei – it's the one with Jalapeno. So good!

Manapua is similar to Japanese nikuman (steamed pork bun). It is filled with Chinese-style barbequed pork (cha tzu) most often, but you can find several flavors of manapua, and it is available at many supermarkets throughout the island.

Loco Moco is another mixed-plate favorite. Normally eaten at breakfast, loco moco is a hamburger patty served over rice and covered with gravy and a cooked egg. Da Kitchen and Zippy's are both known for their loco moco.

Food Trucks on Maui

When Maui initially closed down due to pandemic, many restaurants had to temporarily close, the Foodtruck industry filled the gap. Because they are already set-up for "take out" and "to go", they were naturally the place to go to buy food.

There are many foodtrucks on Maui and I will not attempt to list them all. What I decided to do was to collaborate with Yelp Elite's Top Maui Food Reviewer, the foodie Travis Tagala for him to share some of the best food trucks on Maui.

Travis started his food Instagram @travis.eat to support small and local businesses during this crazy time of pandemic. He found a lot of joy in connecting with businesses, while learning about their stories, and experiencing new foods.

Here are the top 5 Foodtrucks Travis recommend on Maui:

Gestes Shrimp. *Wanna get a taste of Maui's Famous Hawaiian Shrimp? If yes, then Geste Shrimp is the answer! Geste Shrimp is currently located with the pod of food trucks across from the Costco gas station. It's a black food truck with a huge shrimp and the Hawaiian Islands stamped on it.*

Upon arriving, the menu is very simple and straightforward, which is perfect for an indecisive person like me.

My go-to order is their Shrimp Plate ($15) which comes with 12 pieces of shrimp, 2 scoops of rice, and crab mac salad. It's the most craved entree on their menu and is cooked in different styles – Hawaiian Scampi, Hot and Spicy, Spicy Pineapple, Pineapple, and Lemon Pepper. However, my favorite out of the five is their Hawaiian Scampi. Overall, the shrimp is extremely flavorful and the crab mac salad compliments the dish very well. The shrimp is not peeled, which I don't mind one bit. There is open-air seating, but I do prefer to take it to-go and peel the shrimp in the comfort of my own home. Don't forget to bring cash because they are a cash only operation.

Whether you are a tourist or a local, Geste Shrimp is definitely worth a try. Instagram: @gesteshrimptruck

Thai Mee Up. *Thai food on your mind? Another favorite food truck that is also in the Kahului food truck pod across from the Costco gas station is Thai Mee Up! Overall, the portions are very generous and every dish that I've tried so far has always been enjoyable. I love how easy their menu is to read and how they have daily specials, so be sure to ask about it! To top it off, all of their dishes are made FRESH to order and their Kahului location is open from 11am-pm, Monday through Saturday.*

I always order their Pad Thai Shrimp, and I personally think it's the best pad thai on Maui, period. Flavors are there, good sized portions, and always consistent

Fun fact: Well-known restaurateur Guy Fieri visited Thai Mee Up!
Instagram: @thai_mee_up

MoOno Hawaii. *When I think about acai bowls on Maui, the first place that comes to mind is MoOno Hawaii. I've been supporting them since day one when they were first located at the Kahului Harbor. Now, they are located with the other food trucks across from the Costco gas station.*

MoOno is one of my favorite acai bowls here on Maui. I love that their acai bowls here are customizable. Ordering is a breeze – simply choose your size and toppings. You can get toppings based on your preference or you can get it ALL… it's totally up to you.

I always go for their lilikoi butter... which is always a MUST, and their poi, if available.

Be sure to check their Instagram for their location and hours of operation. Their schedule changes weekly, so definitely check Instagram for updates. They have two locations. One in Kahului and another in Kulamalu.

Quick tip for locals: Sign up for their rewards program. It's crazy how fast the rewards add up, the more you visit! I always find myself being awarded with a free premium topping or even a free bowl sometimes.

Instagram: @moonohawaii

Like Poke? *Cue angel singing chorus* Like Poke? is a must-try food truck here on Maui! Another food truck located across from the Costco gas station.

There is a wide list of menu items to choose from, but don't let that scare you. The workers are very friendly and are there to answer any questions you may have.

I usually order their Ahi Katsu or Poke Bake. The Ahi Katsu is a panko breaded ahi with aioli sauce and their Poké Bake is ahi cubes topped with aioli sauce, baked to caramelize, and topped with furikake seasoning. Don't even get me started on their furikake fries. The furikake and aioli sauce complement the curly fries very well.

Of course, if you're in the mood for their classic plate lunches, they do sell raw poké by the pound. I can't stress enough how fresh their fish is. So fresh, the fish melts in your mouth.

Fun fact: They were featured on the TV show Diners, Drive-ins, and Dives. Instagram: *@likepoke*

Sumo Dogs Maui. If you ever see a green and black food truck, with a sumo wrestler holding shave ice in one hand and a sumo dog in the other, please make an effort to try this food truck! For the most part, I've been seeing their truck every week at the Sunday Market at the Old Kahului Shopping Center. This is not your typical hot dog! It's an ISLAND-STYLE HOT DOG!

I finally got to try all four of their sumo dog flavors - Upcountry Guava, Lilikoi Tropic, Maui Mango, and Spicy Onion. Their sumo dogs is a ¼ pound beef Kosher hot dog served on a freshly baked Maui Hawaiian sweet *bread bun, their special garlic and mustard base sauces, and your choice of their island styles sauces. My favorite out of the four is their Lilikoi Tropic! The Hawaiian sweet bread is what makes it 10x better and I love the sweetness of their lilikoi sauce!*

*Be sure to check their Instagram for location and schedule updates. Instagram: Instagram: **@sumodogsmaui***

BONUS for those who like chicken katsu with a twist:

***Sparky's Food Co.** If Chicken Katsu is on your mind, I would definitely check out Sparky's Food Company. They have two locations - one in Kahului, located at 250 Keolani Pl. (next to the Courtyard Marriott Airport location) and another location at the Lahaina Cannery Mall parking lot. It's a white food truck with the big Sparky's logo stamped on it!*

I've tried their Hurricane Chicken Katsu Plate and that was hands down the best! It's Chicken Katsu drizzled with a spicy teriyaki aioli sauce topped with furikake. The plate comes with a bed of rice, corn, and spaghetti salad. The spaghetti salad in particular was very unique only because it's not really common here on Maui as it is on Kauai and the Big Island.

*Instagram: **@sparkysfoodco***

In Addition to Travis's favorite foodtrucks, I would like to add one that's highly respected and recommended by locals:

Maui Fresh Streatery. Kyle Kawakami, the owner of Maui Fresh Streatery was a professor at UHMC and taught there for about 10 years. Kyle pursued his passion and in 2013 opened Maui Fresh

Streatery. It's been a very popular food truck on Maui since its opening. It's known for delicious food as well as community service as he helped serve hundreds of seniors during the pandemic through food distribution projects. Maui Streatry is found every Friday at the Ultimate Air Parking Lot in Kahului. Follow him on Instagram for updated schedule: **@mauifreshstreatry**

For more information on Maui Food Trucks, visit www.amauiblog. com/mauifoodtrucks.com

Sweets and Treats

Shave Ice is not the same thing as a snow cone, as locals will be quick to tell you. Many shave ice companies serve ice cream at the bottom of their shave ice, but traditional shave ice is finely shaved and covered in one to three flavors of syrup; this might be topped with li hing mui powder or condensed milk.

Ululani's shave ice is the most popular shave ice on Maui. I think Ululani Shave Ice is the best. They don't use just sugar water syrup for flavor – their flavors are actually real fruit made into syrup.

Guri-guri is a cross between ice cream and sherbet and is only served at **Tasaka Guri** in Kahului. No trip to Maui is complete without stopping by. This treat is truly loved my Maui Locals because many have wonderful childhood memories associated with it. What is guri guri? Well, it is not exactly ice cream, nor sherbet, nor frozen yogurt, but it's like those three combined. And it is indeed a refreshing treat! They are located at Maui Mall in Kahului.

Mochi is a Japanese rice-flour dessert. Traditional mochi is not very sweet. However, you can find specialty flavors, such as chocolate or butter mochi, all over Maui. Ice Cream Mochi is a variation of this and it is what it sounds like – mochi wrapped around a small ball of ice cream. It is available in supermarkets as well as on several sushi restaurant menus.

Komoda's Donut on a Stick and Cream Puff are super yummy, but there are more! Go to Komoda Store and Bakery and find out. Komoda Bakery is a family-owned business in Makawao which has been around for a very long time (105 years as of this writing). When you're going Upcountry, when sure you stop by this place. It's not a fancy bakery but the treat are delicious! Make sure to go early because they always sell out early.

Malasadas are round Portuguese donuts covered in sugar. There's nothing quite like hot malasadas. It's a doughnut without a hole; a ball of yeast dough fried into perfection – golden brown on the outside and light and fluffy on the inside. Malasadas are best when you eat them "hot" (as in just fried and immediately served). It is usually rolled in sugar but now you can also get them stuffed with cream of various flavors inside. There are many places you can get malasadas. I recommend Sugar Beach Bakery and Home Made Bakery in South Maui, Komodas Bakery Upcountry, and you can also find them at Zippy's in Kahului.

Hula Pie is the most loved dessert at Kimo's and is also available in other T and S Restaurants such as Leilani's, Hula Grill and Dukes. It is a pie made of macadamia ice cream stacked high on Scrumptious chocolate cookie crust. A layer of cool chocolate fudge sits atop of the ice cream, along with whipped cream and toasted macadamia nuts. It is my husband's favorite dessert. We live in Kihei and on special occasions we drive up to the West side to get this treat.

Polynesian Black Pearl Dessert from Mama's Fish House – One of the most photographed dessert on Maui and certainly most beloved too. This lilikoi mouse in a pastry sea shell is a culinary work of art. It is insanely delicious. Available only at Mama's Fish House.

Donut Dynamite – Handcrafted artisanal donuts made from scratch featuring local ingredients such as poi, lilikoi, calamansi and more. Deliciousness at its best. Each donut is made with love and is a work of art by Madam Donut. Located in Wailuku. Place order online at donutdynamite.com then pick up at the shop.

Aunty Sandy's Banana Bread – originally, this delicious banana bread is only available at Aunty Sandy's kiosk on Keanae Pensinsula. It's one of the popular stops on the Road to Hana. When pandemic happened and the road to Hana was closed to visitors, Aunty Sandy and her team pivoted and created a "bake at home mix" of their original famous banana bread. You can now buy them at their foodtruck in that foodtruck place across the road from Costco Gas station.

Maui Cookie Lady Cookies – Deliciously yummy artisan cookies, hand rolled in small batches using locally sourced ingredients when available. The owner Mitzi is one of the sweetest persons you'd meet. This cookie business was started out of love and gratitude (read the story on her website). It is not like a regular cookie, it is huge with decadent flavors such as Kona Coffee Espresso, Pineapple Lychee Passion with Hibiscus Flowers, White Chocolate Macadamia Nut, and more!

Cinnamon Roll Faire in Kihei – Located underneath the Coconuts café at Kamaole Shopping Center, you will find the Cinnamon Roll Faire featuring a small counter stocked with sandwiches, muffins and trays of delectable sticky, gooey, delicious cinnamon rolls. Freshly made every day. You will have a choice of various toppings – I highly recommend the macadamia nuts toppings.

Hula Pie

PERSONAL NOTES AND PLANNING

CHAPTER 7

BETTER SAFE THAN SORRY

Important Safety Reminders

Abide by the Safe Travel Program and Social Distancing Guidelines

You definitely don't want to catch COVID-19 while you are on vacation on Maui. It important to follow the safety protocols and social distancing guidelines. Wear mask properly, wash hands often, keep distance when possible (6 feet apart). Most of the business establishments have sign posted in their places to remind their customer and clients about these safety protocols. I cannot stress enough the importance of this. I understand that in some States, there are no restrictions about wearing masks. But when you come visit Maui, you must abide by Maui guidelines and rules. (June/July 2021 update – Masks are no longer required when outside)

Don't turn your back to the ocean.

When I gave this safety tip on one of my safety posts at our "Visit Live Love Maui Facebook Group", a reader asked "What do you mean? How am I supposed to go back to the shore?". The reader's question is a hint that many tourists who are not familiar with the dangers of the ocean are naive about it. My answer to the reader was "Walk sideways and be aware, or swim back". While walking the shoreline or standing there watching, you never know when a strong wave might sneak up on you. It can knock you off your feet and can hurt your neck or back. In other places like Nakalele Blow Hole, you might get knocked off into the ocean and get sucked far away. You really don't want your fun Maui vacation to become a tragedy for you and your family.

Don't swim in the murky water especially after the rain.

This is the condition when "shark attacks" usually happens. Also stay out of the water at dawn, dusk, and night, when some species of sharks may move inshore to feed. But be aware that tiger sharks are known to bite people at all times of the day.

Check the weather report before hiking. Avoid the danger of flash floods by not hiking where rain is in the forecast.

Never attempt to cross a flooded stream. Keep on the designated paths to prevent getting lost and stranded. It is important to stay on the marked paths at all times; when hiking, bring water to drink, wear a good footwear, and put on mosquito repellents.

Don't leave your car with all your valuables inside.

Maui has relatively a low crime rate but I hear stories of families losing all their baggage because they left it in the car, on the parking lot at Costco (or other grocery stores) because they decided to stop by the grocery store on their way to their hotel. If you must stop and buy something, make sure one of you stays in the car. Same is true the hiking trails or the Road to Hana. Do not leave valuables inside the car as you go our exploring.

Don't drink and drive.

You are on vacation and we understand that some of you would like to "drink and be merry". That is fine. That is great. But here is a friendly reminder: Don't drink and drive! I can't tell you enough how important this is. You may think that in your hometown you can drive even if you had some drinks (which you actually should not do) ... but remember, you are not familiar with the roads here.

Do yourself and your family a favor - when you "partied", just take an UBER going back to your hotel or condo. Avoiding vehicular accident during your vacation is worth paying the Uber Driver.

Protect your Skin, Use Reef Safe Sunblock

Many new visitors fry themselves on day one of their vacation in an overzealous quest for tan. Don't do that. It will be a major discomfort on your trip and it won't be fun. It will also cause damage on your skin. Enjoying Maui's tropical climate means being sun smart and wearing proper sun protection. Even when sun is hidden by the clouds, protect yourself from ultraviolet rays that come through. Before going out for the day, liberally apply sunscreen with SPF (Sun Protection Factor) rating of 30 or higher and re-apply after swimming. It is important to use Reef Safe sunscreen.

Protect Your Eyes, Use Sunglasses

Always wear sunglasses and a hat when you are out in the sun. It is important to use sunglasses with UV Filters to protect your corneas from sunburn and to prevent cataract.

Don't Drown – When in Doubt Don't Go Out

It is a good practice to go out in the water with someone instead of alone (buddy system). This way, you can watch for each other. If that is not possible, and you are going solo, I suggest swimming at the beaches with life guards.

When swimming at unfamiliar beach, ask the life guard about the current conditions (in addition to paying attention to the warning signs at the beach.) Every beach can be both perfectly safe and lethally dangerous depending on the water conditions of the day.

PERSONAL NOTES AND PLANNING

CHAPTER 8

WHEN IN HAWAII, RESPECT AND FOLLOW HAWAIIAN CULTURE

At this time during the pandemic, some visitors developed a perception that "Maui Locals" are anti-visitors. While there are some who are vocal about not wanting visitors, the majority are actually visitor friendly. I found that visitors who knows the basic Hawaiian values and cultures are the ones who enjoy their Maui vacation to the fullest. They not only fell in love with the place, but they also all fell in love with the people.

I enjoy sharing about "things to do on Maui" but I am most humbled and honored to share about basic Hawaiian values and cultures to Maui visitors because I think this is very important. It's not just about going to a Luau and watching Hula, it's not just about learning to say Aloha, and Mahalo. It is much deeper than that. I urge you read this Chapter before your arrival to Maui. That my friends can be considered an act of Aloha.

So here are some of the important Hawaiian values you need to know. This is not a complete list by any means, but I believe that knowing and applying the following values is a good start: Kuleana, Malama, Kokua, Pono and Aloha.

Kuleana

It is a uniquely Hawaiian value and practice which is loosely translated to mean "responsibility". The word Kuleana refers to reciprocal relationships between the person who is responsible and the things they are responsible for.

During pandemic, the practice of Kuleana was evident in the way the people of Hawaii protected their "Kupuna" (elders). Most, if not all, felt it is our responsibility to protect our elders, not just within our ohana, but the whole community as well. Hawaii is one of the first States where mask wearing was mandated and is strictly implemented. People wear masks because we feel it is our Kuleana to do so.

Malama

This value "malama" is closely related to the value of "kuleana". Malama means to tend, to care for, preserve, protect and watch over. To put it together, we can say, "it is our kuleana to malama our ohana and aina. On our previous discussion on Kuleana, we touched about the caring for our family (ohana) and elders (kupuna). In this section of malama, I would like to turn our attention to "Malama Aina".

As visitors to Maui, it is your kuleana to malama the aina. This means taking care of the land, which extends to taking care of the ocean, the creatures and the natural resources.

Here are some of the ways we can put this value into action:

Use a sunblock that won't hurt the reef.

While sunblock may protect our skin from the sun's strong and sometimes-harmful rays, it doesn't protect Hawaii's famed coral reefs. In fact, many sunscreen products contain toxic chemicals that lead to irreparable damage to corals, most commonly leading to a type of damage called "bleaching," in which corals lose their color and die. Many of the world's most beautiful coral reefs have been severely harmed or have completely died in recent years, and researchers have drawn a clear link to chemical-laden sunblock. The good news is that many skin care brands have started to adjust their formulas, and there are also many local, independently-owned, reef-safe sunblock choices to choose from. Using a reef-safe, biodegradable sunblock is not only beneficial to our living coral reefs, but it is also a cleaner, less-toxic choice for our health, too. Typically, the more natural products will be marked with a "reef-safe" sticker or label. In 2021, a new bill will go into effect banning the sale of non-reef-safe sunscreen in Hawaii, which will make the choice much simpler!

Don't throw plastic in the ocean. Strive for minimal use of plastic.

Plastic has become one of the most commonly seen pieces of litter around the world, and the Hawaiian Islands are not exempt from the effects of this. Single-use plastics, like utensils, take-out containers, straws, and plastic bags are often found littering Maui's once-pristine beaches and floating in the waters and around our reefs. Make sure to never throw your plastic (or any other waste, for that matter) into the ocean, and try to limit your use of plastic products. Being mindful of your plastic usage is one small way to maintain accountability and help lower the amount of plastic that ends up floating in our oceans and streams.

Don't feed the Nene

Nene are also known as the Hawaiian Goose, and they are the official state bird and an endangered species whose only natural habitat is in the Hawaiian Islands. They are adorable and sometimes friendly, but if you encounter them during your stay on Maui, we ask that you admire them from afar and not feed them any "human food" for a variety of reasons. For one, it is simply not a natural part of their diet, and the added sugars, fats, and preservatives can be very harmful to the nene's health. Additionally, these rare birds can be accustomed to approaching humans when they are fed, which can be dangerous for both the human and the nene, as the geese may approach unexpectedly or wander into roadways. Lastly, we simply want to keep the nene wild and safe in its natural habitat, without human interference. In the late 1950s, the Hawaiian Goose was nearly extinct as a result of human activity, with only thirty known birds remaining. Thankfully, the nene population has bounced back, but now it is our 'kuleana' (responsibility) to keep them safe.

Don't get too close to the Honu and do not touch them.

Honu, or green sea turtles, are believed to be a sign of good luck according to Hawaiian folklore; however, touching a honu is most certainly bad luck! By state law, it is required that humans maintain a distance of ten feet from wild sea turtles, and intentionally touching a turtle can result in fines of up to $10,000. Of course, there are often encounters that are out of control, and you may be lucky enough to have a honu swim near you while in the ocean. If this happens, be mindful to keep your distance and not touch the turtle. While it can be tempting to shout "Honu!" to the beach, we recommend enjoying the sighting and then letting the turtle continue on its way. Far too often, one person will see a turtle and then a flock of fifteen people will follow the turtle down the coast. This can be incredibly stressful for the turtle, and in many situations, can lead to fines from the Department of Land & Natural Resources.

Don't get too close to the Monk Sea and do not touch them.

The Hawaiian Monk Seal is a critically endangered sea mammal, with only about 1,400 seals known to be in existence. As a result, the seals are protected and monitored to ensure their survival, and there are big fines for touching them or getting too close. This distance isn't just for the safety of the seals, though. On average, Hawaiian Monk Seals are between seven and eight feet long and can weigh between 375 and 500 pounds. They can be aggressive if they feel threatened, and despite their size, they can be very swift in charging at any perceived threat. Law requires that humans maintain a minimum of fifty feet from the seals, and breaking this rule can result in fines of up to $10,000.

Don't litter - pick up your "opala" on the beach, parks, etc.

"Opala" is the Hawaiian word for trash or garbage, and sadly, locals see a lot of opala in places it shouldn't be, including our beaches, oceans, waterfalls, and forests. Maui has so much beauty to offer, and it is shared with millions of tourists every year; however, with increased traffic comes increased litter in some of our most beautiful and sacred places. When visiting the islands, make sure that you are mindful of your trash and belongings. Practice a "leave no trace" mentality when enjoying the many natural resources on Maui, meaning any trash or food waste (even biodegradable items like banana peels) should be disposed of in a proper receptacle. We all have a responsibility to be respectful to the land and to preserve Maui and its resources for future generations of locals and visitors alike.

Don't step on or touch corals

When swimming, snorkeling, or scuba diving, be mindful not to touch the corals. There are many reasons to admire our living reefs from afar, but perhaps the most important is that they are very endangered and rapidly dying or disappearing from our oceans. Simply touching a piece of coral can be incredibly harmful to the entire colony, as human skin contains oils and compounds that can be destructive to the health and stability of coral. The oils can disturb the delicate balance and lead to the death of an entire reef. Additionally, it is important to avoid stepping on corals, as this can kill the small polyps that serve as the foundation of the reef structure. In rare cases, stepping on or crashing into coral can result in a hospital visit, as small coral polyps can get into the skin and continue growing, causing painful outcomes. Lastly, please do not take coral or seashells home with you as souvenirs. The corals and shells are homes for many sea creatures and taking them as ill-considered souvenirs is incredibly harmful to the natural ecosystems that we so admire in Hawaii.

Kokua

The word "Kokua" means "help". Its deeper meaning is to extend help to others in sacrificial way with no intent of personal gain. It is about giving without expecting anything in return. This value is manifested ever so clearly during COVID-19 pandemic on Maui. With very high unemployment rate, many people who had lost their jobs, and many entrepreneurs who lost their businesses needed kokua. The people on Maui generously give. Many supported Maui Food Bank as this on-profit organization oversees the distribution of food to those who are in need to food.

When you come visit Maui at this time, one way to show kokua is by leaving generous tips to your service providers (food servers, room cleaners, drivers, etc.). I understand you are already spending a lot or money coming here to visit, and some of you might be tempted not to give tips. Going the extra mile by practicing kokua will make you a better person on Maui, and beyond.

Pono

Like many Hawaiian words, Pono does not have a one-on-one English translation. If there were one, it would most likely be "righteous" as in the State Motto "Ua Mau ke Ea o ka Aina I ka Pono" meaning "The life of the land is perpetuated in righteousness". A simpler translation of pono is to "do the right thing".

The concept of pono is taught to Hawaiian children at a very young age. It is a guiding principle that is to shape their every decision. "Is it pono?" they are asked. In their words, will what you're about to do help bring harmony and good into the world?".

When you come visit Maui, be aware of the value of pono when making decisions. For example, it is not pono to trespass on a private property.

When exploring the great beauty of Maui, it might be tempting to pursue every hidden waterfall, cool hiking trail, or spectacular viewpoint that you heard about, read about or think might be out there. Please keep in mind that, while the ocean and beaches are there for all to enjoy, some of the methods to access them cross private property and that is not okay to do. You may be able to find an acceptable access point by doing an internet search, or you may choose to move on to the next attraction because there is no end to the fabulous sites to see on.

The word "Kapu" means "no trespassing." When you see that sign, please do not enter that property. It may be tempting, and yes, you may see others who are ignoring the sign, but you are breaking the law and you are being disrespectful and dishonoring to the local Hawaiian's land and you could get arrested. There are countless numbers of fabulous sights to see on Maui that does not involve accessing private, so please avoid doing so. Aside from being illegal, too many people trampling on the land can harm the balance of the ecosystem and ruin the topography and that is not pono. Respect is very important on Maui and it is up to each of us to honor our kuleana (responsibility) to malama (take care) of the aina (land), the kai (ocean), and poe (people) of Hawaii when we visit.

Aloha

When you're in Hawaii, it is very common to hear the word ALOHA. A day won't pass without you hearing it or seeing it. Aloha is probably one of the most used Hawaiian word. And it has a variety of use and meaning. We use ALOHA to say hello and goodbye, we use it as a greeting or salutation on a letter. We use ALOHA for LOVE. But really ... what is the true meaning of ALOHA?

I read an article titled "Deeper Meaning of Aloha" by Curby Rule and the explanation opened up a whole new understanding of the word. ALOHA's deeper meaning is that it is a way of life. Here is an excerpt:

The spirit of Aloha was an important lesson taught to the children of the past because it was about the world of which they were a part. One early teaching goes like this:

Aloha is being a part of all, and all being a part of me. When there is pain – it is my pain. When there is joy – it is also mine. I respect all that is as part of the Creator and part of me. I will not willfully harm anyone or anything. When food is needed, I will take only my need and explain why it is being taken. The earth, the sky, the sea are mine to care for, to cherish and to protect. This is Hawaiian – this is Aloha!

Now that we have explored what ALOHA is, the question is how do we apply in our lives? How do we practice ALOHA? There will be many opportunities for you to express Aloha during your visit on Maui, and beyond.

PERSONAL NOTES AND PLANNING

CLOSING THOUGHTS

Timing is everything.

This book was conceived in 2020, in the midst of the COVID-19 pandemic. By the time I am publishing this book it is July 2021.

I was initially discouraged with the delay of publication. However, in the end, it all worked out and made this book more relevant. The recent July 2021 updates were added just before publication, particularly in the Hawaii Safe Travel update on Chapter 3.

At the time of publication, Maui's visitor industry is "resurrecting". On one hand it is a good thing, especially for our economy. On the other hand, many local residents are ambivalent. "Overtourism" is a concern.

Writing this book was a challenge and a learning experience for me. But it is all worth it. And I am grateful.

If you read this book while planning your vacation to Maui (whether it's your first time or returning), it means to me that you are among the responsible tourists who educate themselves before visiting. It is my hope and desire that you have a safe, pleasurable, relaxing and memorable vacation on Maui.

Mahalo and Aloha,
Liza

ACKNOWLEDGEMENT

This book started with the blog. I owe it to my blog followers to mentioned them first and foremost in this acknowledgement section because without them I probably would not have dared to write this book. So I thank them first.

A Maui Blog followers and friends, thank you. Thank you for loving Maui with me. Thank you for not only subscribing to my blog, but also showing up in social media channels, liking, commenting and sharing. You never fail to express your appreciation of what I do for Maui, and that made me want to do more. (www.amauiblog.com)

Paul Brodie, who's two books on visiting Maui inspired me to write my own. Both books were short and simple. I read them back in 2017 and I thought if I aim for short and simple, I can do it too. Well, this Maui guides book is not as simple as his books, but Paul got me started anyway. *Thank you, Paul, for coaching me on book publishing back in 2017 when I first attempted to write this book. It took longer than usual, but I did it. I now have published a book!*

Judy Ann Koglin, my new author friend. When my original book publisher failed to perform and my book deal fell apart, Judy came to the rescue! I would have given up on writing this book had she not intervene. She held my hand on those discouraging times. She told me I can self-publish, and she helped me every step of the way. She is amazing! Judy learned the self-publishing process during the pandemic, and she published 7 books right after (www.mauishorespublishing.com) Yes, seven! It is all part of the The Guesthouse Girls book series for Young Adult readers. *Judy you are marvelous! Thank you for rescuing this book.*

Karen Johnson, Cassie Kepler and Karene Nakagawa. My "soul sisters". They provide loving support not only on my book writing but in all areas of my life. In this season of my life (first time author), they became my "proof readers and editors". They are talented and flexible like that. More importantly, they are also my prayer warriors. *Thank you, Karen, Cassie and Karene, for your love.*

My colleagues at Wailea Realty: Alana Rucynski, Lydia Pedro and Darla Philipps (www.TopMauiHomes.com), Diane Pool (www.SoldOnMaui.com) Christina Haywood (www.mauichris.com), Jack and Katie (www.teamnicolettisellsmaui.com) and Dale Richardson and Gigi King (www.luxurymauirealty.com) - *Thank you for your encouragement and support. You are among the very best in the real estate industry on Maui! I'm honored that you made a decision to pre-order this Maui 2021 and Beyond Book so you can share them with your family, friends and clients.*

Chris Norberg (MauiInformationGuide.com), Mark Goldberg (MauiGuidebook.com), Jon Bloom (MauiHawaii.org) and John Derrick of (GuideOfUS.com/Hawaii) *Chris, Mark, Jon and Derrick - thank you for your support. Your websites are valuable resources for Maui Lovers. Thank you for always being willing to share your information and knowledge with us, and for allowing me to use some of your articles and maps here on this book.*

Kathy Takushi (www.captivatingjourneys.com) - Kathy is a Maui Island resident and Travel Advisor and Owner of "Captivating Journeys" a boutique Hawaii Travel Agency. *Mahalo Kathy for your excitement to share this Maui book with your Maui Lover clients and friends. It is delightful that we both have the passion to share our love of Maui with the Maui Lovers around the world.*

Lena Castles, founder of VenieBags.com. *Your passion to protect the environment is inspiring. You are the first to financially support this book via my campaign at Publishizer. I can't tell you enough how encouraging that was to me. I wish you the best on your goal to continue offering sustainable products that help to keep our planet green and healthy.*

For our Hope Chapel Ohana group with the Maucks, especially Beth Sedestrom, for praying for me and the success of this book. *I love it every time I hear your prayer for my book during our Ohana group. Thank you for your constant encouragement.*

Stacy Small, founder and owner Elite Travel, for graciously writing the Foreword on this book. *Thank you for your kind words.*

To the Members of Visit Live Love Maui Facebook Group - *Thank you for always showing up, for your posts, for helping answer questions, and simply for loving Maui with me.*

To my family - my husband Brad, and our children, Gardner and Noelle. *Thank you for your love and for being my family.*

Thank you to all of you who are reading, or have read this book. May this book be helpful to you and may you have the best Maui Vacation ever! Mahalo for choosing to read this Maui guide.

Last but not the least; actually, the most important: Thanks be to God who enabled me to finish this book and get it published.

TOP MAUI HOMES
We specialize in you.

Thank You to Top Maui Homes for their generous support in the publication of this book

www.topmauihomes.com

LAST BUT NOT LEAST

Resources

Reading this book is a great start on planning your Maui vacation. Because changes also happen, I would like to share with you these online resources that I know are helpful and valuable. I have used these resources as well while I am writing this book.

WEBSITES:

COVID-19 on Maui and Hawaii:
   https://hawaiicovid19.com
   https://www.mauinuistrong.info

Visiting Maui Information:
   Maui Information Guide - https://www.mauiinforma-
      tionguide.com
   Maui Guidebook - http://mauiguidebook.com
   Hawaii Guide (Guide of US) - https://www.hawaii-guide.com
   Maui Hawaii - Jon Maui Guide https://www.mauihawaii.org
   Go Visit Hawaii - https://www.govisithawaii.com
   Go Hawaii (Maui) - https://www.gohawaii.com - https://
      www.gohawaii.com/islands/maui

Hawaii Activity Authority - https://activityauthority.com

The Road To Hana - https://roadtohana.com

Haleakala Crater - https://haleakalacrater.com

Maui Photographers - https://hawaiiphotography.com/

Molokini Crater - https://molokinicrater.com/

Haleakala Crater - https://haleakalacrater.com/

Maui Luau - https://mauiluau.com/

Maui Whale Watch Tours - https://mauiwhalewatchtours.com/

Maui Accommodations Guide - https://www.mauiaccommodations.com

Maui Blog - https://amauiblog.com (look for the page Maui 2021 and 2022 update where I will continue to add the happenings that affects travel and visiting Maui, including Safe Travels Program, Opening and Closing of Restaurants and local businesses.)

YOUTUBE CHANNELS:

The Hawaii Vacation Guide - https://www.youtube.com/c/TheHawaiiVacationGuide

Maui Travel Video - https://www.youtube.com/c/MauiTravelVideos

BKR - https://www.youtube.com/c/BKRVlogs

Maui Guide - https://www.youtube.com/c/MauiHighlights

Visit Live Love Maui - https://www.youtube.com/c/VisitLiveLoveMaui

Active Tours (Maui Playlist)- https://www.youtube.com/watch?v=8FeNDxiZFxo&list=PL8ldRrW72LEsOIuHG-Sp8vMIsWOYmz0fGg

Yellow Tours (Maui Playlist) - https://www.youtube.com/playlist?list=PLOVadUHX1B-JiIlHp_9RgZPkLQ2KGsKnO

PODCAST:

The Aloha 360 - https://www.thealoha360.com

The Hawaii Vacation Connection Podcast – https:// www. hawaii-aloha.com/podcast

INSTAGRAM:

There are many Hawaii and Maui focused Instagrammers. These are a few I recommend you follow if you love seeing photos and videos on and about Maui.

@amauiblog   @mauimemories

@MauiHI   @bridgettlovesmaui

@VisitLiveLoveMaui   @thealoha360

@mauibelle   @malikadudley

@CarolsMauiLife   @mauiair

@MauiInfoCollector   @archershoots

@mauimorning   @dan.brandes

@allaboutmaui   @tutuspantry

Planner and Sample Itinerary (Free Download)

At the end of every chapter of this book I have provided a space for you to write notes. You can then turn your notes into your personalized plan or itinerary.

If you desire to see a sample plan and itinerary, please go to www. amauiblog.com

Bulk Discount

Are you planning a wedding on Maui and would like to give this book as a gift to your guests? Are you a corporation giving incentives to your Top Performers by sending them to Maui for an all expenses paid vacation? This book is a good gift to give prior to their trip. Are you a travel company who may want to give this book as a gift to your clients traveling to Maui? For bulk discounted pricing, please order at www.amauiblog.com